TAKE COVER!

TAKE COVER!

Spike Webb

Copyright © Spike Webb

Proudly published by the author

Published in 2020 by the author.

Copyright © Spike Webb

The author asserts their moral right under the Copyright, Designs and Patents Act, 1988, to be identified as the author of this work.

All Rights reserved. No part of this publication may be reproduced, copied, stored in a retrieval system, or transmitted, in any form or by any means, without the prior written consent of the copyright holder, nor be otherwise circulated in any form of binding or cover other than that in which it is published and without a similar condition being imposed on the subsequent purchaser.

A CIP catalogue record for this title is available from the British Library.

Names of people and schools have been changed to protect the privacy of individuals.

PROLOGUE

The Villiers Arms. There it was, perched on the junction of two roads that carve the niche in which this friendly hostelry stands. As I turned the corner into Villiers Road that Sunday afternoon, it appeared like a beacon that beckoned as I quickened my step in eager anticipation of camaraderie, laughter and fine ale.

On entering I was greeted by a few friends already gathered at the cosy bar near the roaring fireplace.

'Ahh! Greetings Mr Webb – some splendid drumming yesterday by the way!'

'Thanks…'

'Tch! Tch! What nonsense – he was utterly useless.'

'Aww…'

'Abysmal! In fact, I have never witnessed such a complete catastrophe. It was nothing short of embarrassing for all who were unfortunate enough to be present at the time.'

'Really? Oh dear…'

'Yes, a total shambles. What's it to be? Side Pocket for a Toad?'

'Yes, pint of Side Pocket please.'

'Incidentally, do you know where that name originates? It is an old saying that alludes to things being useless, so your choice is entirely appropriate!'

'A bit like a chocolate teapot?'

'Precisely.'

'So the manufacturers are effectively saying that their beer is pretty well useless?'

'Indeed…'

'They must have harboured a deep and sure understanding that it is, in fact, the opposite.'

'Quite so – have you had any luck on the job front this week?'

'No, nothing solid. Still doing my evening cleaning job!'

'Well, it's something I suppose.'

'I'll tell you what, you'd be amazed at what people leave behind in the toilets.'

'Eh?'

'Oh yeah – food wrappers, even food scraps!'

'Really?'

'All over the floor. It would appear some people like to eat while sitting on the toilet.'

'Urgh! How bizarre!'

'There's one person who's particularly fond of hard-boiled eggs.'

'Really?'

'Yes, I often come across bits of eggshell on the floor by the pan.'

There's a mixture of convivial laughter and disgust. Then someone else joins in:

'I think I'd choose a scotch egg if I was having a snack on the bog.'

'Why's that?'

'It seems a lot more sturdy somehow, less fiddly.'

'A cleaner operation in fact.'

More laughter. Soon it's time for another round and I'm presented with another Side Pocket.

'Weren't you a window cleaner for a while?'

'That was back in the summer, helping out a mate who does rounds in posh areas. Problem was, he had to let me go eventually.'

'Why's that?'

'I'm afraid of heights.'

More laughter.

TAKE COVER!

'I could only do the ground floor windows with a short ladder. Sometimes even that got a bit scary on some of the higher windows. He found it funny at first – used to say he couldn't believe he'd employed a window cleaner who was terrified of heights and nervous of ladders!'

'So nothing from the recruitment agencies then?'

Nah! December's the worst time to get work in the ad or marketing world – everyone's packing up for Christmas. I've been getting emails in my in-box from an online copywriting site called copify which lists small little writing tasks you can sign up to for ridiculously low pay.'

'No, you don't want to be doing that, you need a job.'

Then my friend has an idea.

'Hey, you did that teaching course didn't you?'

'Yeah, the one-month TEFL crash course teaching English Language back in February – couldn't get much work. It's all mainly abroad in places like Thailand – great if you want to be nomadic and travel around.'

'But you got the qualification, didn't you?'

'Yes, passed the course and the final exam at 87%!'

'So you're technically a qualified teacher?'

'Yes, to an extent.'

'Why don't you have a word with Dick? He's just packed in a job as a supply teacher at High Bush School. He's had enough, but it might be something you could do for a while!'

'What kind of teaching?'

'Not sure. Ask him. Look, he's over there, just come in!'

I decided I would, but not before buying my round, which I could only just about afford...

CALL-UP TIME

I've had a number of varied jobs and occupations over the years. Some fabulous, some dull, some vile and some plain bizarre. During those years, there has been one particular activity that I have indulged in from time to time when the need arose: cleaning. It can be hugely unpleasant, especially if you're cleaning toilets. But, as many cleaners will tell you, it can also be hugely therapeutic. Getting rid of day-to-day rubbish, the disposal of detritus, making floors shine and even removing total strangers' excrement from white porcelain can be strangely cathartic.

So I didn't mind when at fifty-six years old, having got over the initial anticipation of this, I found myself cleaning office facilities, in particular the toilets, from six until eight every weekday evening as a way to bring in a (very) small income. It had been over twenty-five years since my last foray into other people's mess, but I remembered it with some fondness, and anyway, I needed the money.

Trouble was, I needed more money. For some months this was my only source of income and the meagre savings I had were quickly diminishing. My freelance work as a copywriter/content writer had dried up and I was getting too old to be applying for flashy jobs in advertising like I use to have. I make a little money on an ad hoc basis as a drummer, but you can't rely on it.

But I had to pay the bills, and I like to drink Guinness with my wife and friends in my local in the evenings, so I

TAKE COVER!

needed my little cleaning number to become a supplement to another income as opposed to my only one.

Then, one Sunday lunchtime, I was chatting to some friends in another local of mine. They were being very generous and standing my round as they knew I was struggling. It was generally decided that relying on occasional freelance work with some drumming thrown in was simply not good enough. It turned out that one of my companions, an ex-policeman, had been working as a cover support teacher at a particularly troublesome local secondary school, or academy as some are now called. He was very pleased because he was about to pack it in. He'd had enough. Apparently this school's students (which is how you must refer to them these days) were extremely challenging.

However, he recommended it as something I might like to consider as I had become qualified to teach English Language to foreign learners the previous year as the result of an intensive one-month course at a college in London. Since then I hadn't had much luck finding work teaching foreign students and I had become despondent. But teenagers? It can't be that bad, surely? And cover support isn't actually teaching or planning lessons. You just hand the work out that's been left for them and supervise in the teacher's absence. Of course, the money isn't great, but it's something – and I could keep my cleaning job in the evening.

He said all I needed to do was Google 'Cover Support teacher roles' and specify my local area town and opportunities would appear.

So, after a little trepidation, I did...

MY FIRST DAY AT THE FRONT

I'm at the back of the bus on the way to my first assignment as a cover support teacher at a school called Gatesbury. I note how buses still seem to jolt as sporadically and violently as they did when I was at school. It's a blustery day outside and occasionally my window is pelted with fresh raindrops, interrupting my view as I peer through the glass to watch the world go by in the Monday morning gloom. It's also cold out there and I'm grateful for the warmth of the bus, which is about half full. There's a musty smell in the air, as though the bus is still warming up and ventilating after a long night in a damp garage.

Taking the bus is my only option as I don't drive, so I'm watching as stop by stop it fills up with school children. They range from year 7 to Year 11, which means roughly 11 to 16 in age. Some are tired, probably having hurriedly wolfed down a breakfast cereal before gathering books, bags, coats and saying a quick goodbye to Mum and Dad, or maybe just Mum, or just Dad. Some on the other hand are chirpy, even cheeky, full of beans.

For my part I'm a bit of both. I'm tired because I'm not used to getting up at 6 in the morning, and I certainly can't eat at that time. But to get this bus, which gets me to school at 8.30 in time for my cover briefing, I must first catch a 7.29 train at

TAKE COVER!

the station which is 20 minutes' walk from my house. So I'm tired.

But I'm also a bit chirpy, because I've been building up to this for a while now. Having had a successful meeting/interview to become a Cover Support Teacher with a supply teacher recruitment agency, I had to attain a CRB check in order to work in schools, which can take a few weeks. Mine came through more quickly than expected, but I still had about a week to mull over what it might be like to stand up in front of a load of teenagers and tell them what to do. I went through all the usual self-doubt, telling myself I must be crazy as I've had no experience with kids. Ok, so I've taken lessons teaching English Language to foreign learners during an intense TEFL course a year ago, but that's nothing like this. This is scary.

I've been reassured by the agency that cover work does not involve the actual teaching of a particular subject, it is rather the delivery of pre-set lessons. So, if you are to cover a maths lesson, for instance, the necessary lesson plan and related work exercises will be waiting for you. All you have to do is give out any materials and tell the class what they are supposed to be doing and then, of course, make sure they do it. Naturally, if you find yourself covering a lesson that happens to be your subject (in my case English), then you can use your initiative and help by answering questions or even entering into discussion. But basically, you are there to cover for the absent teacher. And the bottom line is, you must remain in the room at all times.

So I came to the conclusion that I must embrace the challenge, try and make a difference if I can. If the kids don't want to do the work, I must try and persuade them that at the end of the day, it's the best thing for their future. Knuckle down now and you won't regret it. I've even got plans to be a bit quirky and spend some time at the beginnings and ends of lessons talking about what they enjoy doing and what they might want to do for the rest of their lives! That might get their interest.

So I'm fairly nervous but at the same time a bit chirpy.

SPIKE WEBB

The bus drops me right outside the school and we all get off together. I feel a bit like one of them, except this is my first day. I want to get it out of the way and suddenly I get that sinking stomach feeling and can't wait for home time when I can run indoors and tell my wife all about it over supper and a glass of wine.

A bit like a lost child, I look for signs to reception, but decide to ask a group of children/teenagers to save time.

'Just over there, round the corner to the left!'

They smile sympathetically. Well, I am a new boy after all.

* * *

On introducing myself at reception, I receive a similar smile of sympathy as the lady behind the desk gets me to sign in and gives me an ID badge. After a while the Cover Support Supervisor arrives and directs me to the staff room and says the cover work folders will be with me shortly. I am given a school itinerary brochure with details of lesson times, breaks, school rules, disciplinary procedures, Consequence and Reward structures and fire drill.

The staff room is large, populated by many hardback sofas and chairs and features a kitchenette area to one side as you enter. Here, you may help yourself to tea and coffee after putting 20p into a money slot tin on the counter top. I fancy a cup of coffee but feel a bit too new and shy to go for it yet, so I sit down and peruse the school brochure as teachers and support staff pour into the room. The room gets very full very quickly with about 50 people and I realise that this is a pre-school staff meeting as someone in authority, who I assume is the head master, stands in position about to address everyone. A young man dashes over and plonks a purple folder down on the small coffee table in front of me. And without so much as a smile:

'Your cover work for the day!'

The head master speaks of this and that, singles out a few teachers to give their own messages and updates to the assembled crowd and after about 10 minutes, he signs off:

TAKE COVER!

'Have a good day everyone, hopefully without too much stress!'

Everyone laughs.

I'm concerned now though, because the bell's about to go and I haven't had a chance to make head or tail of what I'm supposed to be doing and where. There is a list of names for each class on individual cover sheets that I must tick off when I take the register. Each sheet has a grid of coded information along the top, giving essential details of which period it is, what year group, what subject, the name of the classroom and the exact lesson times. The trouble is, I've never seen one of these before, and to make matters worse the type is really small, so I need to fumble in my pocket for my plastic reading glasses from Poundland before I can make any progress.

There goes the bell. And I haven't even got as far as the contents of the cover work folder yet! I'm panicking, and everyone else is in a hurry to get to their own lessons so I can't ask for any help. Eventually I manage to work out where I'm supposed to be: M3, in the maths block. I rush to reception and ask the way. While traversing various quads and covered walkways I look inside the work folder for the appropriate lesson plan instructions; only to find that there isn't one for period one. So I refer back to the cover sheet with the names and notice for the first time it has a message scrawled on it:

Work in classroom on desk.

A BATTLE OF WITS

I'm struggling to read the instructions on the cover work sheet that has been left on the teacher's desk. This is partly because I'm using my cheap, Poundland reading glasses which tend to blur my vision and also because I'm distracted by the noise. 25 thirteen-year-old kids can make quite a racket when they haven't yet been told to be quiet, something which I'm warming up to. I've never told 25 teenagers to shut up before and I'm wondering about the best approach. Shall I be stern from the start? Take no nonsense? Make a quick example of someone? But that would be unfair wouldn't it? Perhaps I should be calm and kindly, like a favourite uncle, allow them to warm to me? Or maybe somewhere in-between? Nice but not to be messed with? Firm but fair?

The trouble is, the longer I take over looking at the cover brief (which is written in a hurried scrawl which I have trouble understanding) and deciding upon my stance before taking a compulsory register, the more noise they make. And sometimes they get daring.

'What's your name, Sir?'
'Where's Miss Leigh?'
'You look like Rod Stewart!'

I should mention that, over the years, my career as a drummer has seen me develop a hairstyle that is spikey and a bit messy. I've always liked that slightly modish look, however I don't actually look identical to Rod Stewart and have no intention of attempting to copy his image, iconic though it is as

TAKE COVER!

a reminder of one of British pop/rock music's most magical eras. I can hardly blame students for noticing the somewhat unusual countenance of a new cover support supply teacher who does, in fact, look more like an out-of-work rock musician.

Anyway, it's definitely sink or swim time, so I take the plunge. The water's going to be cold, it'll be a shock at first but once I get moving it'll all go swimmingly. I opt for more than a little volume.

'Good morning everyone, my name is Mr Webb!'
'Morning Sir'

Well that's a start. I need to keep talking though as some of them are clearly in the mood for chatter and jolly japes. I decide to implement my rehearsed strategy.

'I'm going to take a quick register to establish who's here. After that, we're going to spend five minutes talking about something other than school work.'

They seem vaguely interested in this unforeseen deviation as I start to read out the names on the form register. Plenty of Courtneys, Tylers, Tyrones, Josh's and Jacks I notice. Some of the surnames are difficult to pronounce but it seems Christian names suffice (unless there are two the same). Sometimes, however, I come across a Christian name belonging to one of our multi-cultural brethren that I don't know how to pronounce. I do my best, but my mispronunciation is always met with much mirth and laughter. I smile apologetically which only helps to re-affirm the class's correct assumption that I am going to be a bit of a pushover.

As I look up after finishing the register I see several hands in the air accompanied by earnest offers to take the completed form down to student services, as it must be delivered there before the lesson begins.

'Me and Courtney can take it down for you, Sir!'
'No, me and Josh'll do it!'
I decide to be decisive.
'Tyler, you take it down please.'
'Can Courtney come with me?'
'Why?'
'It'll be quicker with two of us Sir!'

SPIKE WEBB

Whilst I admire their attempt to persuade me that two people carrying a piece of paper will actually speed up the delivery process, I insist that Tyler will take it on her own.

'Oh Sir!'

'Two minutes maximum!'

Tyler leaves the room slightly disappointed but nevertheless triumphant that at least she gets to leave the class for a short while.

'Ok everyone, before I give you your set task for today, we're going to spend five minutes talking about what you did last night!'

Looks of bemused amusement all round.

'Courtney, what did you do last night?'

A slight giggle.

'I watched Eastenders and went on Facebook.'

I point at a lad at the back.

'How about you?'

'I played football in the park.'

'And you?'

'Not much really.'

I realise that last night is only Monday and no-one will have much to talk about, so I abandon the subject.

'Ok, onto today's maths task, which I believe is algebra. I'm going to ask you to complete exercises 12 to 14 in your text books...'

Courtney's mobile phone rings. As she answers it, I am acutely aware that mobile phone use is forbidden in class.

'Allo? Oh, I'm wearing my bright blue Converse sneakers!'

'Er, excuse me Courtney...'

'I had to change into them cos my Addidas trainers got soaked!'

Everyone's looking, some are giggling.

'I think it's about time that conversation ended Court...'

'Hang on Sir...no I'm wearing my Contessina Ankle Boots tonight!'

'Come on Courtney!'

TAKE COVER!

'Ok, sorry Sir.'

She says goodbye and puts the phone away. As I give out the text books, I realise that everyone is seated in pairs and groups that offer the best opportunities for lively, social discourse, as if in anticipation of an hour's fun and laughter. The problem is, the seating plan that was left for me on the teacher's desk is no real use as I've had no opportunity to get to know who's who, and there are no photographs to go with the names. Besides, moving people around now would only result in more moaning, groaning and over-zealous protestations which I don't have the stomach for. And anyway something as decisive as that clearly has to be addressed at the start of the proceedings when, if at all, you set a precedent.

I start to walk around the room, going amongst them, looking over shoulders to make sure they are applying themselves to the task. There's a noise from over in the corner. A white boy and an African girl are fighting over a pen. I approach, with a masterful countenance.

'Thank you! Can we get on with the work please?'

'She took my pen Sir!'

'I did not – why would I want your stupid pen?'

'You nicked it!'

I remember being told never to take sides.

'I don't care who did what, get on with the work please…'

There's a struggle and the pen ends up on the floor at my feet. I'm tempted to pick it up, but what then? Who do I give it to? The alternative is to tell one of them to pick it up, which would be a worse act of favouritism. I pick it up and put it down quickly on the white boy's desk. Cue the African girl:

'Sir that's racist!'

'No it's not – now stop messing about with pens and get on with it…'

I walk away as I speak as if to affirm my last word on the subject and the official end of the pen affair, only to spy three girls at the other end of the room huddled over a mobile phone, all with in-ear headphones on, nodding heads in time to music. I instinctively redirect my pace towards them in a movement not unlike the automatic reaction of a pre-programmed toy army tank.

'What has this to do with Mathematics?'

They look up, apparently surprised. One girl removes an ear piece.

'Pardon Sir?'

'Mobile phones away please…'

'But Sir, Miss Leigh always lets us listen to music to help us concentrate!'

I take a second to ponder this. Then, as if right on cue, the other two remove their ear pieces and re-affirm in unison:

'She does Sir!'

I'm inclined to think that musing over the finer points of algebra and all the complex formulae that lie lurking within probably can be enhanced by a few soporific, ethereal trance vibes. But my instinct tells me that they are probably listening either to aggressive rap music or modern romantic rubbish by the likes of Justin Bieber. I fire my main gun.

'Sorry, mobile phones away.'

'But Sir? !t helps us concentrate!'

Like hell it does. I fire again.

'I said, mobile phones away please…'

I mentally reprimand myself for saying please. I remember the same person who said never take sides also telling me I should never say please. Looking dejected, they put their phones away. I turn to see a hand in the air. Someone has actually put her hand up to ask a question. She seems perplexed:

'Sir, I don't understand the question?'

'Which question is that?'

'The first one – exercise 1.'

I know nothing about the finer points of algebra, but nevertheless feel compelled to at least look at the question and in so doing I discover that I don't understand it either. I'm about to tell her that I know more about zebras than algebra when there's a crash from the back of the room. I turn to see a boy giggling on the floor, having fallen or been pushed off his chair. Several others are laughing hysterically. I mobilise

TAKE COVER!

myself towards this new area of conflict. The rest of the class, or rather those who aren't otherwise engaged in conversation, are waiting to see what I intend to do, as indeed am I.

I play for time by firing a question:

'What's going on here?'

'He pushed me off my chair Sir!'

The accused puts his hands up in mock disbelief at this apparent bare-faced lie.

'I didn't Sir…'

I remember that thing about not taking sides.

'Up you get…'

The boy gets up as slowly as possible amid much mirth and merriment.

Someone else decides to throw something into the mix:

'Sir that's physical abuse – he should get a C4 for that!'

I should, at this point, explain that secondary schools nowadays have a points system by which teachers must issue punishments when going about their duties administering discipline. These are displayed in great detail on a huge 'Consequences' chart on the wall of each classroom, alongside a similar 'Rewards' chart which operates in reverse, depicting reward points for good behaviour and exemplary academic achievement. Students seem to pay little attention to the latter, concentrating rather more closely on the disciplinary side of things. In fact, they seem to have exerted themselves in the study of the consequences chart, so much so that most of them know it off by heart and would pass a GCSE with flying colours, if one existed.

'That's definitely a C4 Sir!'

The accused raises his hands again in disbelief that he could be so randomly selected as the assailant:

'Sir, I never…'

I go on the defensive:

'I don't have time for this, settle down all of you and get on with your work please!'

SPIKE WEBB

I turn to see someone else with his hand up. I sigh inwardly at the thought of having to confess to knowing nothing about algebra when he surprises me:

'Sir, I'm bored!'

'What?'

'These are too easy – I've finished!'

I look and discover that he has answered every question in exercise 12. I adopt an expression of surprised admiration but also point out that he needs to continue on to exercises 13 and 14, to which he emits a long and painful groan, a bit like someone might do on being told they have appendicitis:

'But Sirrrr! It's sooooo boring!'

'I know – just get on with it – come on, you'll be finished in no time.'

He seems encouraged at the thought of it all being behind him soon and resigns himself back to the text book. By this time though, the noise in the classroom has reached an almost unbearable and certainly unacceptable level, so I need to fire more guns.

'Thank you everyone – let's keep the noise down!'

I mime the word down with my arms for emphasis, which works to a degree, although the topics of conversation are clearly far too fascinating to be abandoned completely and I'm far too tired and frustrated to go for all out war and demand complete silence. Just as I'm congratulating myself on effectively lowering the noise level, a figure saunters past in the form of a tall young man on a mission.

'Excuse me – where are you going?'

He seems surprised, but answers helpfully, as if giving directions to a lost passer-by:

'To sharpen my pencil over there at the bin, Sir.'

'Oh...ok then'

I'm acutely aware that I'm becoming too much like Sergeant Wilson in Dad's Army. I need to deploy a bit of Captain Mainwaring:

'But don't be long!'

'Ok Sir!'

TAKE COVER!

That's better. I watch him for a while, impressed at how long someone can spend affecting the repair of a blunt pencil, the need for which I didn't have the energy to question in the first place, when I allow myself to steal a look at the clock on the wall in the hope that there's not too much time to go before the bell goes. I discover to my dismay that there is half an hour to go, to which I emit an inward groan not unlike that of the algebra student earlier.

Suddenly there's an exclamation behind me. I turn to see that several boys have regrouped into a foursome around 4 desks which have been pushed together. As I approach, one speaks to assure me of their noble intentions, nodding reassuringly:

'We're going to help each other with the work, Sir! We'll get it done quicker that way...'

I turn back into Sergeant Wilson.

'Well, anything that helps you get the work done is a good idea I suppose.'

Then I notice one of them has his phone out and is on Facebook. On seeing me approach he quickly changes the screen and reassures me:

'I'm just going to use my phone calculator to help with the answers...'

Cue the others:

'Miss Leigh lets us Sir!'

Cue Captain Mainwaring:

'You can only use the calculator – no going on Facebook or anywhere else!'

'Ok Sir!'

Just as I'm about to take another turn around the room, survey the battlefield again, a girl approaches, clutching her stomach.

'Sir, can I go to the toilet?'

I remember being told to watch out for this one. I look at her with sympathy:

'No. I'm afraid not.'

'But Sir I really need to go!'

SPIKE WEBB

'Sorry, you'll have to wait – there's not long to go now anyway...'

(I wish.)

'Seriously Sir I'm in pain!'

'Sorry, no.'

She turns to go back to her seat, again a bit like someone with an unpleasant disorder of the intestine. I glance back at the group of boys to discover that they are, in fact, in the middle of a card game. I'm about to put a stop to their little game when there's another crash at the back of the classroom. I know what's happened before turning to look. It's the same lad on the floor again, but this time the performance is even more elaborate, as might befit a sequel or reprise. The same boy who played the part of the accused already has his hands up, wearing an expression of highly amused disbelief that he could be wrongly accused yet again. As I'm teetering on the edge of either losing or keeping my temper, I turn away briefly only to be confronted again by the same earnest toilet seeker, now with an even more exaggerated look of agony on her face. She is a first-rate actress pleading with all her heart for one tiny little visit to the toilet.

Amid all this commotion on this highly charged battlefield that masquerades as the study of algebra, I am momentarily reminded of my obligations later in the day, when I will be taking solace for two whole peaceful hours in some toilets of my own in an office block back in Watford. It's my part time, early evening cleaning job, and one which, on reflection, no longer seems like a necessary chore, but rather a haven of blessed retreat.

I glance at the clock. Five minutes until the bell. A hitherto quiet student spies me doing this:

'Sir? We're allowed 5 minutes to pack up!'

Even as he says this he is pulling his coat from the back of his chair. And right on cue, everyone follows suit. But it's one battle I am inwardly delighted to lose as I have seriously had enough. Technically, I should wait for the bell to go before letting them out of the classroom but the consequences of keeping them in for another 4 minutes, left to

TAKE COVER!

their own devices, are far too horrendous to contemplate. So, resigned to their partial victory, I walk towards the door. This ignites a fuse, an excitement that travels from the front of class right back behind the lines to the mutinous infantry at the back. Along with the others, the toilet seeker gets up with her coat on, no longer in agony, but rather calmly looking forward to her burst of freedom before the next performance.

And it is a performance. Me included. We are all cast in this absurd farce that is a battle of wits, a tale of random consequences, all cleverly choreographed with impeccable timing. I open the door, quickly and decisively, as one who fires a starting gun. The collective war cry of teenagers set free from their incarceration is accompanied by the echo of chairs banged and scraped on the floor, a final blast of artillery fire to celebrate victory and herald the coming of another unwanted lesson. I feel nervously guilty at having let them out early. I wonder what the authorities at the school might think about that. But then, what are they going to do? Fire me?

Or give me a C5, perhaps.

BACK AT BARRACKS

I'm in the staff room during morning break time after my first two lessons. I'm a little shell-shocked as I hadn't realised just how stressful it would be. I'm also feeling a bit shy as I don't know anyone, so I've plonked myself down on the same spot as before at the end of a long seating area, away from the general hubbub. I've been brave enough to help myself to a much-needed cup of coffee in the kitchenette area. As I sip this gratefully, looking through folders containing cover work for some of the day's remaining lessons, I realise what a lonely business this is. I'm new here, not a permanent, regular fixture, so making friends is a bit of a no-go area. I feel a bit like I did on my first day at big school, shy and nervous and wondering if I'll eventually get to know anyone.

A teacher wanders in looking more than a little weary. Someone inquires as to her health:

'You Ok?'

'Just about – had a particularly horrible Year 9 class just now!'

'Oh dear, poor you – you came out in one piece though.'

'I don't know what's got into them – they're impossible today.'

As I'm beginning to wonder just what I've got myself into, the bell goes and it's time to make my way to another classroom.

BEHIND THE LINES

All morning I've been wondering what Ashfield's school is going to be like. I've heard it's very rough – the Ashfield's estate has a bad reputation. How will it differ from Gatesbury? That's pretty rough itself. One of the unnerving aspects of this job is never knowing what people or circumstances you're going to encounter. And if, like me, you've had little or no experience in dealing with difficult classroom situations, you aren't armed with a selection of practical and acceptable approaches to deploy as and when applicable.

So here I am at Ashfield's in the afternoon, covering an hour of English for a class of Year 8s. That means second year in traditional terms, aged 12 to 13. I can hear them gathering noisily outside the classroom as I'm looking at the cover work. I took advantage of it being lunchtime and came into the room early to get a head start as I'm still quite new to this. It turns out they have been reading and studying a novel about a homeless bloke who spends some time in prison. He eventually gets let out on the streets again and gets befriended by another homeless person, but comes unstuck again when that person disappears. It sounds like pretty serious stuff and judging by the sound of the mob gathering at my door, not what they are in the mood for. But it's not actually for me to judge. The work has been set. They are to draw or design a new front cover for the book, based on their own personal impressions of the story and the characters within. I'm quite pleased with this because getting 12-year-olds to put pencil to paper to draw something is probably a bit easier than getting them to write.

I look up to see one young lad has entered the doorway and is flicking the lights on and off deliberately to annoy me. I decide to ignore him and usher them all in. They are followed by a stern-looking classroom assistant whom I recognise from the staff room but have never met. She says a brief hello and I get the impression she is from somewhere in the Ukraine. She has a vacant and slightly cross look about her as she takes up a position at the back of the room.

As always, the students occupy seats that are best positioned for close friends and partners in crime to enjoy a good old social and, as my modicum of experience has taught me, the assembled class will not remotely resemble anything like the predetermined seating plan outlined and usually insisted upon by their proper teacher, a copy of which has been left on her desk. The problem is, although I have a list of their names, I do not know what names to put to which faces in order to successfully move them around the room. Of course, I can study the seating plan ever so closely at the same time as taking the register, but they can then simply pretend to be each other. They are also very good at protesting, claiming that all kinds of changes and modifications have been made to what is an ancient and outdated floor plan. In essence, If I attempt to mix it all up and change people round at random, I'll be starting something. I'll have become the bad guy before I've even begun.

I take the register, periodically calling for quiet as I do so. Then comes the usual discussion about who takes the completed register down to Student Services.

'I'll take it, Sir!'

'No let me – I'll be quicker!'

'Let me and Holly take it, Sir!'

As I select someone called Grace to do the honours, there's a commotion at the back of the room. An unkempt looking girl called Taylor is standing up defiantly and chewing gum in the kind of way that indicates her intentions for the foreseeable future. I'm not sure what has occurred, but she is

TAKE COVER!

clearly also upset about something. The stern looking assistant is standing near. I approach and calmly ask her to sit down, which she does. I make a mental note to watch out for her during the course of the lesson.

I put my hands in the air and gesture grandly for quiet before explaining that they will be designing a new front cover for the book they've been reading about the homeless person who went to prison. They seem reasonably happy with this as they rummage around for pencils and pens etc. As I'm giving out blank sheets of paper for them to draw on, I decide to chat a bit about the book to show some interest in their task because, after all, this is something I can actually contribute something to, help them along even:

'So the main hero in the story is homeless and then ends up in prison does he?'

'Yes and he finds a friend but he gets killed…'

'Is it a good book?'

'No, it's fucking crap!'

A little startled, I see that Taylor has spoken. Someone else protests:

'No it's not, it's good!'

'It's crap – I'm not doing this!'

Technically, I should give Taylor a C3 for swearing in class and a C4 for refusing to do the task, but I'm thinking there must be a better way to calm her down. I'm about to try and diffuse the situation when standing up, Taylor throws something else into the mix:

'My dad went to prison!'

The others don't agree.

'No he didn't…'

'Oh yes he fucking did!'

I can tell by the look on her face that she's not messing around. She's dead serious and not happy about it either. A C3 seems about as relevant as a P45 right now.

'Ok everyone, calm down and let's see some great new front covers for the book you've been reading.'

I go over to Taylor who has sat down again.

SPIKE WEBB

'Come on Taylor, you might not like the book but I bet you can draw as good a picture about it as anyone else – better even!'

She seems placated, but not entirely happy. But my attention is distracted by some boys at the front of the class. It's the pencil nicking thing again. What is it about 13-year-olds and pencils? I go over to sort it out, which seems to take forever as I have to try and restore order without actually taking sides. The problem with the issue of theft and three or four really good actors is if you don't actually witness the incident you'll never get to the bottom of it. And why would you want to? It's not as though it's a wallet that's been stolen.

After I eventually manage to get them back to their cover designing, I notice a lad sitting on his own at a desk near them. He is staring down through floppy hair at the table top, looking morose and horribly alone. I decide to leave him alone and move around the room for a while. I go over to a girl who has her head resting on the desk, also looking ahead with a look of boredom combined with frustration on her face. I later learn that her name is Olivia. She has scrawled a load of lines across her piece of paper, the would-be canvas for her book cover design. I decide not to ignore this:

'That's interesting…'

She looks up, as if expecting a bollocking.

'What you've done there represents exactly how you're feeling right now, doesn't it?'

She nods.

'It means you're bored and want to get out of here, you want to escape.'

She nods again, a little more enthusiastically.

'But what's even more interesting is it's the same as how the main character in the book you've been reading feels. He wants to escape too, from being homeless and from prison.'

I've got her full attention now.

'I tell you what, if you can draw his face behind those squiggled lines, that would represent his character in the book really well. Give it a bit of shading as well and that could turn out to be the best book cover design in this classroom!'

TAKE COVER!

To my delight Olivia picks up her pencil and gets to work.

After another turn around the classroom, during which I note that the aforementioned boy staring down at his desktop is still looking lost and lonely, I'm alarmed by another outburst from Taylor.

'Fuck off! Go away!'

She is addressing her displeasure to the foreign teaching assistant who is standing over her, having attempted to calm a situation that had evidently been brewing for a while. The assistant approaches me and remonstrates:

'Sir, she must be given a C4 and sent from the room – this behaviour is unacceptable!'

I walk over to Taylor.

'What's going on Taylor? You can't swear like that in here!'

'I don't like her Sir – you're alright but I don't like people like her! Keep her away from me, she's fucking mental!'

Cue the assistant:

'You must send her out!'

Taylor decides to take the law into her own hands, throws her book in the air and gets up to leave the room:

'Fuck this, I'm going anyway!'

She saunters out of the classroom, slamming the door as she goes. I ask the assistant to find a suitable person from Student Services to collect Taylor from wherever she wanders to and detain her in the designated exit room assigned for such purposes.

The rest of the class have been a little unhinged by this. Some are giggling, some have even cheered a little, others look on with distracted interest. Soon, however, I manage to restore order and get them back on task. The good news is they all seem to quite like designing their book covers and it gives me the opportunity to encourage them individually and collectively. As I'm doing this, I glance over to check on the lonely staring lad with the intention of asking if he is ok, but I see that my group of pencil squabblers have invited him onto their table and are helping him with his cover design. Whatever was upsetting him I'll never know. It could have been bullying from someone else in the school, it could have been a row at home, anything. But he's ok now, thanks to the boys on the next table. I'm warmed to see such an example of basic human compassion on this battlefield. Sometimes I wish those guys would show the same degree of sympathy for cover teachers, but why should they? I get paid for what I do and I get to go home to a happy existence. That poor boy has to be here and may well have to go home to an unhappy existence.

I'm distracted by a burst of general laughter and look up to see that Taylor has managed to avoid any potential captors and found her way to the area outside the classroom windows at the back, where she is sticking two fingers up to the whole class, grinning as she does so.

Two fingers to the lot of you.
Two fingers to the stupid story.
Two fingers to my dad.
Two fingers to the world.
Two fingers to the breakfast I didn't get this morning.

This angry 13-year-old's certainly cross about something, but what exactly is anybody's guess. After a while she wanders off as it's getting near bell time.

I start to collect up the cover designs, showing some particularly good ones to the class as I do so. Then, as it's nearly time to go, I go over to see what Olivia has done and am delighted to see she has drawn the face behind the squiggled lines just as I suggested, with a little shading for added effect. She looks up, smiling:

'What do you think Sir?'

'Very good work, excellent – you've turned those squiggly lines into something really good. In my opinion that's the best design in this classroom. Well done!'

The bell goes and with a smile on her face she runs out with the rest after carefully putting her picture in her exercise book.

TAKE COVER!

It's home time so I can make my escape. I pick up my bag and coat from the staff room, make my way down the staircase and out through reception.

'Good night!'
'Good night!'

On the way out towards the school gates I blend in to the mass of teenagers on their way out. All with their own lives to go to, their own agendas, their own ups and downs, joys and disappointments, highs and lows. And when the bus finally arrives at the stop up the road, I board with a weary nod to the driver as I show my return ticket and make for a back seat near a window. As it moves off to begin the long journey home, I stare vacantly out of the window. I'm very tired, and the events of the day have become a bit of a blur. I'm a little confused, overcome with fatigue. I've got jumbled memories of another long day, aching feet…

…and some squiggly lines of my own.

SOLITARY CONFINEMENT

It's lunchtime and I'm wandering alone along a pavement just down from Gatesbury School. To my left is a busy main road and to my right are open fields. Someone's walking a dog in the distance. I take out my sandwiches from the depths of my Dad's old great coat. I like to wear it at the schools; not just because it's warm, but also because it's big and carries a certain authority with it. My Dad often had a stern countenance and I wanted a little bit of that. And, of course, it reminds me of him and that's comforting.

I hungrily open the tin foil wrapping. My wife has made these sandwiches for me; lovingly, just like my Mum used to when I started big school 47 years ago. I like to eat my sandwiches as I stare across the fields, alone. Just like I did during morning break as an 11-year-old boy. Although back then it wasn't fields I stared at, but fifth formers. I would leave the hustle and bustle of the classroom and quadrangles and go to one of the upper year form rooms in the Music block. At the back of the room were dozens of chairs all packed up high towards the ceiling. I would climb to the top at the back and eat my sandwiches in secret while watching the teenage antics of my long haired heroes. They'd play the piano and generally mess around for 20 minutes while eating their own break time snacks.

I did this initially because I was too shy to want to eat in front of my classmates back in the classroom or in the playground. For some reason I felt the need to be alone. After a

TAKE COVER!

while, I became fascinated by these older boys, their self-confidence and apparent worldliness. I decided I wanted to be like them. They must have wondered why on earth I was staring at them every day. They never said anything. Occasionally they would look up and nod and I would nod nervously back from my vantage point near the ceiling. I remember on one occasion returning to this spot having been away from school for a week with mumps and one of them commenting:

'Nice to see you back'

Of course, as the months went on I made some friends and began to behave normally, hanging out in the classroom or on the school fields. Strange then, that my need to be alone while eating sandwiches has returned now I'm back at school. Most of the other teachers and cover support staff enjoy their break and lunchtime food in the staff room, but I have exiled myself onto this lonely road to eat them in secret. I've made friends with a few fellow Cover Support Teachers who I'll probably chat to briefly on my return over a quick coffee, but for now I must continue with my self-imposed solitude. And today I have no heroes to stare at, just the open fields with a man and his dog.

As I turn to walk back, I'm musing over what a frightening place school can be. Not just for shy people, but everyone, young and old. And going to big school must be the first place where you realise just how terrifying it is to be a human being. I'm thinking how hard it must be for some of those people in there, students and teachers alike. The place is awash with fear, pride, anticipation, disappointment, frustration, laughter, tears. In the classrooms, the quadrangles, the corridors, the staff rooms. Just like it is in colleges of further education, in offices, hospitals, on building sites, in sports arenas, concert halls, on street corners, in government departments, on battlefields.

But this is where it all begins. I had forgotten how important homemade sandwiches are. And just like all those years ago, I'm always pleased when they are made with soft boiled eggs.

BACK AT BARRACKS AGAIN

I'm in the staff room again at Gatesbury. I've been coming to this school on and off for a few weeks now and I've made a friend. She's a very nice Irish Cover Teacher who has a fascination for languages. We often sit together at break times and compare notes on the classes, students and varying degrees of seemingly impossible behavior. She's not here today though, so I'm eavesdropping on the conversations over yonder in the adjacent seating area usually occupied by the more permanent teaching staff. They discuss the students, individuals who are a particular problem, or whose parents present problems. Sometimes they talk about other stuff like food, dieting, babies, dogs and if it's someone's birthday, cake will be involved. They are a tight unit and seem to support each other as a matter of some importance, which is understandable because their jobs are difficult and very stressful. When they talk about their concerns for certain students, they are their real selves and I feel I kind of know them.

But I sometimes wonder what they think of me. This Cover Support Teacher with slightly messy hair who hardly speaks and never eats. Sometimes one of the Teaching Assistants is in my cover lesson, which is when they witness part of the real me as I try and reason with difficult students. If they see me lose my cool with a persistently badly-behaved student and send them out, they've seen what I'm like when I'm

TAKE COVER!

a bit cross, which is actually quite personal. In real life, nobody but my wife knows what I'm like when I'm a bit cross, which isn't often. But these people get to see my real self too, or at least the self that communicates with students and occasionally gets exasperated.

So it strikes me as odd that when we're back in the staff room, we don't communicate. It's not a problem as I've discovered that the shyness I had as a new boy at big school has returned as a relatively new Cover Teacher. I'm not the kind of person who can plonk himself down amongst them all confident like:

'Thought I'd start hanging with you guys as I've been treading the boards here for a while now!'

Of course, it makes sense for the Support people who come in on an ad hoc basis to sit separately; it's a kind of natural divide. When my Irish friend struck up conversation I was reminded of the feeling I got when someone first spoke to me when I was a new first year at school. It gave me a lift just as it did all those years ago. Usually, in real life I'm quite gregarious and confident, totally the opposite of shy. But in this school environment all my insecurities have returned.

Just as I'm musing over what it might be like to be accepted over there with the big crowd, talking and eating with confidence, the bell goes to signify the return to lessons and it's time for me to go off and be a grown-up again.

CLEANING THE MESS

It was Friday afternoon and the first day of my new job. I was scheduled to be working as a cleaning operative at an office building in my hometown of Watford. My hours were set at 6 until 8 every evening, during which I would be found mainly in the toilets on both floors occupied by the company plus the reception area and adjacent canteen. I hadn't done this kind of work for some years due to my activities as a copywriter in advertising among other things, and was a little apprehensive. Sure, I remembered mastering the use of cleaning materials, solutions, cloth variants, mops and mop buckets, bin liners and vacuum cleaners called Henry, but I wasn't sure what technological developments I might encounter after 25 years out of the game.

    I went into the reception at 5.50. After all, it's good to show you mean business on your first day. The man who had interviewed me and a couple of others the day before came out and introduced me to Darren, who was going to show me the ropes before introducing me to Fizz, my general supervisor. We took the lift up to the first floor (although this would not become my regular choice as the stairs are a good deal quicker). We walked past an open-plan office area where a few late workers glanced up from their computer screens, presumably checking out the new guy. Then through some (soon to become very annoying) fire doors and onto a corridor lined by 4 doors. Darren showed me into each in succession.

TAKE COVER!

The first led into a small shower room complete with towel rail. The next was a men's toilet comprising three cubicles, a twin urinal area with adjacent full-length mirror, three wash basins in front of a large vanity mirrored wall area, two wall-mounted antibacterial soap dispensers, a modern-style power hand dryer and, as you'd expect, a large municipal metal flip-top waste bin with an attractive chrome finish.

The ladies was almost identical but with the added advantage of an extra cubicle (four in total) and an extra wash basin. Darren opened an additional door next to cubical 4 and gestured grandly to a cleaning store which contained everything I would need to go about my duties, the first of which would be to replenish the soap dispensers and, most importantly, the toilet rolls in the cubicles.

I saw this as a way of easing me in slowly before getting down to the nitty gritty.

Darren then took me to our final port of call on the first floor.

'Oh, and there's this.'

He opened the door to another room at the end of the corridor which turned out to be a toilet for disabled people, uniquely designed to accommodate associated special requirements, one of which featured the inclusion of no less than three toilet roll holders, cleverly positioned at various levels on the wall next to the toilet seat itself. One helpful hint was to be always aware that the third and lowest positioned loo roll was located so low down that it was generally out of a standing person's line of vision, obscured as it was by the wash basin, which was of course placed unusually but conveniently nearer to the toilet itself. So this could be easily overlooked when attempting to furnish the room with a full complement of fresh toilet rolls.

There then came some detailed instruction with regard to cleaning solutions. This confirmed my prediction with regard to advanced technology in that good old-fashioned bleach and detergent had been disposed of in favour of a new product. This was apparently super eco-friendly and was organised in a colour-coded system. Green for floors, blue for stains and pink for surfaces including basins, toilet seats, bowls and rims. However, the green could also be used for basins and even toilet seats at a push, should the pink run out.

After a few days on the job, having been left pretty much to my own devices, I discovered that it didn't matter a shit what substance one applied to what surface as it didn't seem particularly substantial in practice. I spent the first few weeks splashing a combination of green, blue and pink (mainly pink as there was more of it and seemed to be a general favourite) all over the place to pretty much little or no effect. The cleaning company were, however, particularly proud of this new acquisition and always quick to extol the ecological virtues of the substances.

'Totally harmless! Just wipes off your skin with a piece of loo paper!'

On one occasion, the man who originally interviewed me, the MD of Brownlow & Sons, returned to check on things and attend to some special cleaning requests in another part of the building. He entered the ladies (I always started in the ladies as it coincided with my initial visit to the cleaning store where I pulled on my rubber sanitary gloves) as I was wiping down the vanity mirror to remove the stains.

'How's it going?'

'Not bad, getting into a routine.'

He held up a plastic bottle of the pink stuff.

'How's the surfaces? This stuff doing the trick?'

'Well…'

'You've got to remember, it's specially made to work over time. Spray plenty around when you start and give it time to work.'

'Yeah sure…'

'It just keeps on penetrating – even when you've finished cleaning.'

'Really?'

'Oh yes, but it's also completely harmless to people. Watch…'

He then proceeded to squirt a good measure of the pink stuff into his mouth.

TAKE COVER!

'See? Harmless!'

And with that, he left. I couldn't help wondering as to the substance's potential. If, like the man said, it continues to penetrate deeply after use, what is the point? If I've cleaned an area sufficiently, surely that should be the end of the matter? But even more curious was the demonstration of how ineffectual it is under other circumstances. If it's harmless on the inside of your mouth, what possible harm can it do to a stained loo seat or a blob of excrement clinging to a toilet bowl?

Perhaps the most extraordinary thing I discovered over the first few days was the habit Fizz had of eating her dinner in the toilets. One evening, I hurried into the walk-in cleaning cupboard in the upstairs Ladies to find her preparing a pasta and tuna salad in a plastic food container, next to the cleaning materials and sanitary glove boxes in front of the large, bumper toilet roll packs.

'Don't mind me, just having a spot of dinner!'

'Sure, hungry work cleaning!'

I swiftly collected a pack of bog rolls and made my way to the Gents down the corridor. As time went on, I found that Fizz did not confine her dining arrangements to the cleaners' cupboard. I regularly happened upon her perched on the wash basins opposite the cubicles themselves, dangling her feet back and forth over the edge while eating a boiled egg with a salad bowl on her lap.

Then, on one occasion, I was vacuuming the floor in a Gents toilet cubicle when I saw a pile of discarded egg shell. I thought no, she can't have been eating her dinner whilst actually on the toilet? My suspicions were confirmed one evening when I was cleaning the toilet bowls in the Ladies cubicles. I was hurriedly going through my routine; having earlier sprayed a load of pink stuff round the inside and under the rims of the bowls to give it time to do its job while I changed the toilet rolls in their holders, I was using my paper rags, wetted with tap water, to scrub all the crap away before chucking them into the big metal bin. I was acutely aware that the middle cubicle door was closed. Just as I was thinking it might be best to vacate the Ladies and start in the Gents then come back when whoever was in there had finished her business, Fizz's voice piped up:

'Don't mind me, just having a bit of dinner – I'll be finished in a minute!'

I mumbled something about needing to finish off in the disabled toilet and went to start in the Gents. It may not have bothered Fizz but it somehow troubled me to be throwing about all those effluent germs while she ate her dinner.

Mind you, I was often surprised to see discarded food in the toilet cubicles. It seemed that some office staff had taken to consuming vittles in the bogs as well. Many was the time I would clear up pastry crumbs, chocolate bar wrappers, plastic spoons with what looked like yoghurt residue (or maybe ice cream?), and of course, egg shell and egg white.

Sometimes I asked myself: Am I missing something here? I wondered if eating in toilets had become a kind of trend. Perhaps things have changed since the days when I worked in an office. Have toilets become some uniquely universal celebration of the combined consumption and disposal of food? I started taking the idea to ridiculous extremes, imagining office staff arranging after-work jollies in the bogs themselves.

'There's a bit of a do in the Gents tonight after work – bring a bottle!'

The occasional knees-up in the Ladies. Push the boat out and enjoy cocktails and canapes in the Disabled.

But I could never really get comfortable with the idea. Call me old fashioned, but I've always preferred to eat my evening meals as far away as possible from places reserved for the eventual excretion of the food. And even if someone sent me into the toilet to eat my dinner as a punishment, the last thing I would choose to eat is eggs.

LOOSE CANNON

I'm about to cover a morning registration at one of the rougher schools in my catchment area: Ashfields School. That means I am to preside over twelve teenagers of fifteen/sixteen years of age. They are gathered in their form room for twenty minutes until lessons begin; when they will disperse to various other classrooms. I recognise some of them from when I was here last week. I've introduced myself, taken their names and they are chatting nice and quietly as young adults can do when they are relaxed and have no reason to do otherwise. So I'm casually standing at the teacher's desk, looking down and perusing my cover sheets for the day ahead.

      Suddenly there is a loud thud, the sound of wood on wood. I jump in surprise and look over at the direction of the sound. A young man is holding his back and looking round at the person sitting alone at the desk behind him, who has kicked his desk from behind. At first, I'm thinking here we go, surely they haven't started messing about already? I quickly realise that the problem is one of a very different kind. The individual sitting on his own is clearly consumed with rage. He bangs his fist down on the desk with a deafening thud, then he lets out a yell of fury as he bangs it again. Then he gets up, picks up one end of the table and with another scream crashes it down to the floor, before picking up a chair and smashing it down on to the table. He's very strong, and people become stronger when they go completely mad, which is what is happening here. Petrified, everyone makes room for him as he moves across the classroom towards the door, bashing chairs and tables as he goes with all the force he can muster.

I am acutely aware that I am supposed to be in charge here, and having not been previously briefed or trained in the restraint of a dangerous person, I am at a loss as to what to do. I'm also even more acutely aware that I'm only paid about 10 pounds an hour, slightly more than I get as a cleaner, and certainly not the kind of money that would reasonably require me to enter into unarmed combat of any kind. As for the art of reason, he is clearly not in the mood for me to be threatening consequences. And anyway, what kind of 'C' am I supposed to give him? A 'C' for 'Call the Cops?' A 'C' for 'Clamp him in irons?'

Luckily, he crashes out of the classroom, slamming the door behind him. I see that he encounters a female teacher outside in the corridor who seems to know him and attempts to calm him down as she takes him away. I address the silent class:

'Has he done that before?'

'Oh yes Sir, a few times now!'

They declare this fairly casually as though it's just another day in a state penitentiary system out in America's Midwest. Later, on leaving the school at home time, I mention this incident in passing to someone at reception. They seem to know him:

'Oh yes, that's Karl. He suffers from some condition – can't remember the name.'

'Does he go mad regularly?'

'Oh yes, he's put his fist through a plate glass window twice now. Last week he was rushed to hospital with his hands and arms covered in blood!'

On the way home I'm thinking the poor bloke probably has some kind of emotional repressive disorder like Asperger syndrome or something. But what about the poor people who have to be in the room with him? What if he decides that inanimate objects are not as satisfying to destruct as real people? Do the authorities completely understand the nature of this unfortunate individual's malaise?

TAKE COVER!

When I was at school, if a teenager attempted to smash up a classroom, that would probably be the last you ever saw of him, because he would be removed for the safety of everybody else and treated for his condition in an appropriate establishment. As it stands, this guy is a fuming madman, forced into uncomfortable circumstances he clearly can't handle; with the potential to turn into a very dangerous person indeed. Leaving a walking time bomb to hang out in a place with several hundred other people at close quarters is surely a bit of a gamble to say the least? There could be any number of reasons why they do not remove him, but five will get you ten it's something to do with his human rights.

So to recap, if you really don't want to be somewhere, you may as well make it quite clear. Don't mess about making paper airplanes, stealing pens or pretending you need the toilet. Just smash the place up, far more effective.

And no-one will dare give you a consequence. The only consequence will be that you get out of there more quickly than everyone else.

DANGEROUS EXPLOSIVE

I learned something new at school today. There are things called multiplagons. They are to do with maths and feature in the GCSE course. A multiplagon is a triangle that has a circle at each corner with a number in it. In between each circle, in the middle of each connecting side is a square box, which also has a number. Put simply, multiply any two circles and you will get the number in the square between them. In a maths test or learning exercise, these multiplagons will appear with certain numbers missing, so you need to use your knowledge of multiplication, your times table, in order to work out what the missing numbers are. Although very easy at first, they become harder as you progress through the exercise. It starts off as a simple exercise and becomes a bit of a teaser. It is not daunting, over-challenging or arduous, just a fun way to get you using your maths.

So I'm in a maths classroom at Ashfields School, waiting for a group of Year 10 students who are to be given a double-sided sheet of multiplagons to complete in one hour. The task couldn't be simpler to instruct and it's a small group, so I figure I'm in for a reasonably peaceful time of it.

Before long the students stroll in. These are 14 to 15-year-olds, ten of them. I can see immediately that they are problematic and they look as if they are out for trouble. Three of them are on disciplinary report and hand me their report sheets. They all sit next to their favourite allies, positioned for battle. Only one sits alone and she has an assistant support

TAKE COVER!

teacher sitting with her whose job it is to help her with her work. This one isn't trouble, she's just troubled. Troubled by the fact that she can't mix with the others and has trouble understanding simple things.

I introduce myself, take the short register and give out the multiplagons. A couple of students look at them with contempt:

'Sir we've done these before, they're boring!'

I try to stay positive because in the absence of anything else to give them I have no choice:

'Well have a go at them anyway, see how quickly you can do them!'

There's a large girl sitting at the centre of the main group of about 5 to my right who hasn't even picked up the work sheet. That's because she's investigating something on her mobile phone, something which is also of interest to the others around her. I sigh inwardly as I move over to them with my usual remonstrations about mobile phones in class, to which she responds, without even looking up:

'Wait a minute, just let me finish looking at this.'

I'm about to insist that she puts the phone away when the boy sitting next to her bangs the desk underneath with his knee. He then takes out an empty water bottle and hurls it at someone a few yards away, who hurls it back. Of course, if I attempt to intercept the bottle at any stage I will have become part of a game of piggy in the middle, so I feign astonishment and raise my voice:

'Enough of that thank you!'

A couple of kids to my left have actually started doing the multiplagons and, needing a distraction, I go over to see how they are getting on. After all, I'm no mathematician but I'm confident I can help with these, or at least join them in the task. They seem to respond to this, but this is short lived as there's a commotion back at the noisy table. The large girl has had a tiff with the bottle thrower next to her and there's been some kicking of chairs and arm slapping. The boy's face looks particularly vicious as he reddens. Then, surprisingly, he puts his head down into his folded arms on the desk. The girl nudges him and the others goad her:

'You've upset him now! What's the matter Jack?'

I once more appeal for calm and gesture to the work sheets:

'Come on, these are easy. Even I can do them and you lot should be better than me!'

I glance over at the Teaching Assistant who looks up and smiles. Her special needs student looks vacant but comfortable, happy that she has someone special to look after her in this little pocket of hopelessness. Jack still has his head down in his arms which is a bit worrying. What exactly has the girl done to upset him? I go over and decide to show some genuine concern:

'Is he actually ok?'

This falls on deaf ears as they restart their goading. The girl grins and reintroduces her phone into the mix. I look at my watch to see how much longer this agony has left to go when there's an almighty bang. Jack has bashed the desk again and is play fighting with the girl. For one so previously upset he seems to be in relatively good spirits as he stands up and re-launches the plastic water bottle across the room. At this, I've had enough and make a hasty approach:

'Right, that's enough – outside!'

He doesn't seem particularly bothered by this and moves towards the door. But as I attempt to close the door behind him, he has his foot jammed on the other side so that it won't close, trapping him in the doorway.

'Sir the door's jammed!'

'No it's not!'

As I'm pulling at the door handle, another two boys get up and come to the door to assess the situation and, to the amusement of all and sundry conclude that the door is indeed jammed. One of them adds more weight to their argument by putting his own foot behind the door beside Jack's as a reinforcement. I'm beginning to lose it:

TAKE COVER!

I am now the subject of complete ridicule. If this was Basil Fawlty with Manuel and some rowdy drunken guests it would be funny.

'You know as well as I do that this is a perfectly functional door – now get back to your multiplagons!'

But this isn't funny.

Then, to my relief Jack decides the joke's over and leaves the room. However, my relief is short-lived as he begins to bash his forehead on the glass panelled window strip on the door. As he does this, he reinforces the sound by bashing his foot against the door at the bottom, so it looks as though he is smashing his head really hard against the glass. I'm aware that this is attention seeking on a big scale, but the look on his face is one of real anger. I'm getting seriously worried. The Teaching Assistant is too:

'Would you like me to fetch SLT Sir?'

I would, but quickly decline the offer:

'Thank you but not just yet.'

Instead, I decide to ignore Jack and re-establish myself with the multiplagoners to calm things down. After a short while, to my total astonishment, Jack re-enters the room, sits down and, with quiet enthusiasm, starts working on the multiplagons. Everything settles down. The girl is still obsessed with her mobile phone, but I simply can't be bothered with her any more. After a while I move over to where Jack is beavering away at his work sheet. He's already done loads, possibly more than anyone else and I'm genuinely impressed. I don't want to crowd him, so I move away before declaring to the class:

'Hey Jack's really good at these! Come on everyone there's only five minutes left and he's going to end up doing more than the rest of you!'

Now I am truly relieved.

But just before the end of the lesson, Jack exhausts his enthusiasm for multiplagons and begins banging his fist on the desk. The girl is concerned:

'Jack you shouldn't do that you'll hurt your hands!'

'Don't care.'

'But you'll damage them!'

'Don't give a fuck!'

I decide to interject in a somewhat unusual manner. I show Jack my hands:

'I've been a drummer for over forty years. Look at these fingers. They're swollen and damaged. I can't close them properly sometimes. That may be the result of drumming and arthritis. But surely it's better to end up with damaged hands through something like drumming rather than simply bashing your fists on a piece of wood?'

Jack looks interested, but bashes his fist into the desk once more:

'Don't give a fuck!'

Luckily, the bell goes and this little moment in time is brought to a close. On my way to the bus stop I'm winding down, musing over what really went on in that classroom. A hotbed of power struggles, attention seeking, abject indifference, moments of real fear and humiliation, respite followed by ultimate defiance. A time bomb waiting to go off. It's an afternoon I'll never forget. And I've learned something...

Multiplagons certainly have their uses.

HEAVY FIRE AT THE FRONT

I'm about to cover a 1-hour English lesson in one of the prefab huts at the back of Gatesbury school. It's period 4, just before lunch, so I'm a bit tired as it's been a long day already. Still, this class is Year 7 so it should be nice and comfortable. 11 to 12-year-olds can be a bit excitable, but they are relatively easy to control and sometimes quite sweet really. I'm scanning the pre-planned lesson instructions and I can hear the class gathering outside. They sound very noisy, a bit fired up. Then, without being invited to enter the classroom, a few start to crash in:

'Hi Sir! What's your name?'

'I'll tell you in a minute – sit down please!'

In seconds, a mob of 25 have rushed into the room and have, as ever, arranged themselves in the best possible positions to achieve guaranteed fun and high jinks. This class is completely new to me, so I have no idea who normally sits where or with who and there is no seating plan as this is not their usual classroom, and I haven't got the energy to negotiate all the complications that go with splitting them up at random. Anyway, they all seem quite excited to be here so maybe it'll be just fine after all.

As I'm taking the register, I notice a young lad sitting to my right at the front with two other kids. He seems unable to sit still and has a very loud voice, plus a fondness for mischief.

SPIKE WEBB

But this fondness is mixed with a kind of real anger – something I can't quite put my finger on. His name is Liam and he is definitely one to watch. I begin to instruct them about the piece of prose I'm about to give out for them to study and make notes on:

'You need to study this and then...'

'Sir, we always read first!'

My interrupter is a cheeky looking girl a couple of rows away out front. She's holding up a novel type book with an earnest expression:

'We always have 5 minutes reading first, Sir!'

There is nothing on my cover lesson plan to indicate this and nobody else has any reading books out.

'Well sorry, not today – we're going to get straight on with the work! Who wants to help me give out the work sheets?'

Usually there are a number of people keen to help as any excuse to get out of a seat for a while is always welcome. But on this occasion, no-one seems bothered. In fact, they have all engaged themselves in conversations of their own. The reading fanatic has forgotten all about her book and is chatting with people on a table behind her. I decide to hand out the sheets myself as quickly as possible before explaining what they need to do. Some take them with what seems like genuine gratitude, others deploy a bit of sarcasm:

'Ooh thank you Sir!'

It takes longer than anticipated as I'm inundated with requests to go to the toilet – many more than usual. I have to explain that if I granted these requests we would end up with more people in the toilet than in the classroom.

When I finally get back to the teacher's desk, the noise level has risen to that of a fairly loud children's party, so I have to employ a little volume:

'Quiet everyone! Thank you, quiet please!'

This has a small effect, enough for me to give out the instructions in albeit a high and slightly screechy voice. We're now 10 minutes into the lesson and I know it's not going to be at all easy. This lot are a force to be reckoned with. Then something breaks out at the front to my right. Unsurprisingly,

TAKE COVER!

it's centred around Liam, who looks cross. A lad sitting next to him is giggling, but at the same time accusing him:

'Sir? He stole my pencil!'

Liam is passionately indignant:

'I did NOT!'

I move over, ready for battle.

'Liam, come on...'

'I did NOT TAKE IT!'

I look at his accuser, who looks at me with an amused grin:

'He's always doing it Sir!'

Liam yells:

'He's just trying to get me into trouble!'

While this is going on, the noise level in the classroom has risen again, as the rest have resumed their lively social discourse and become doubly animated in the process.

I'm thinking this really is SOME party:

'Alright everyone, that's ENOUGH!'

'Sir I need my pencil back!'

'Why do you need it so badly right at this moment? Just sort it out with Liam afterwards – I've no idea who's pencil it is anyway!'

'It's mine and I want it back!'

Liam bellows fiercely:

'I never took it! It's mine!'

'Right Liam. That's a C3!'

Now he's even wilder:

'That's not fair!'

I have no choice but to diffuse the situation and end this pencil business:

'Liam, go outside!'

'Why? It's a lie – I never took his pencil, it's mine!'

'Just stand outside by the door and cool down!'

He goes outside and, making sure he hasn't wandered off, I close the door and turn to the rest of the class, many of whom haven't even noticed Liam has been sent out.

'Right everyone, I want to see you all applying yourselves to the task in hand! It's not difficult...'

SPIKE WEBB

A large, cheerful but cheeky looking girl shouts out with her hand up:

'Sir can we help each other?'

I'm thinking well that's better than partying:

'Of course you can help each other with the work – let's just see you getting on with it!'

Then there comes a persistent banging on the classroom door. I open it with an inward sigh of anticipation. Liam looks furious.

'I didn't take his pencil Sir – it's not fair!'

He looks upset and I feel almost sorry for him:

'Liam, I'm not saying this is all your fault or that you're necessarily to blame. This is not your punishment, I've just sent you out to calm things down.'

He looks dejected, but placated. I decide to relent:

'You can come back in now, but no more…'

'No, I want to stay out here to cool down!'

'Liam, come back in!'

'No, I'm staying out here!'

The noise level back inside is getting unbearable.

'Ok, have it your own way!'

I close the door leaving Liam red faced and looking genuinely hurt. His companions seem to find the whole thing hilarious. I look at his accuser quizzically, but he is adamant:

'Sir he's always doing it – he steals pencils all the time!'

I look round to see Liam clowning around at the window in the door. Confused as I am by all this, I am then distracted by the commotion at the back of the class, where a young girl is crawling on all fours under the tables. I rush over. I move quickly as I seem to be losing whatever cool I had when this lesson started. It turns out that the unfortunate girl has not only had her bag stolen, but has been goaded for the last 10 minutes as it made its way around the room, passed around by her cruel tormentors.

'Sir, I'm just trying to get my bag back! It's got my phone in it and everything!'

TAKE COVER!

She seems genuinely worried, although she also finds the whole thing almost as amusing as the perpetrators of the crime. I figure the easiest way to deal with this is to locate the bag myself but that proves almost impossible as there are dozens of bags under the tables anyway.

Meanwhile, I'm distracted by two boys at the front left who have decided to play some kind of arm slapping game which is getting out of hand. I rush over to calm it down:

'Hey, that's enough of that! Pack that in!'

Then I remember Liam is still outside. I go and open the door. He still looks red and miserable but smirks at the same time.

'Right you, come back in and no messing around.'

He sits down with the others but his calm behaviour is short-lived to about 30 seconds as the pencil argument resumes almost immediately. Now the chaos in the classroom is almost unbearable. The notion of anyone doing any work long gone, I finally lose it and bellow at the top of my voice:

'Right that's it – ENOUGH! SILENCE!'

To my astonishment, Liam has now stood up and is also shouting at the top of his voice:

'Yes! Everybody SHUTUP! JUST SHUTUUUUUPPP!'

I turn to him in exasperation and yell at him to sit down, but he doesn't. He just keeps shouting. He is as wound up and frustrated as I am. Two of us standing next to each other, 44 years between us, shouting into this mayhem that is supposed to be an English lesson. We're both right in the thick of it, together. Two people who span over 4 decades caught up in the middle of what has become a deafening riot, not knowing where to turn.

So this is it. Complete and utter chaos, where no-one really knows what is going on, or who is on who's side. It's a complete free for all, every man for himself. I look round and spot a hitherto cheeky and bespectacled youth with his head tilted back, laughing hysterically like a battle-worn foot soldier driven insane by the sheer madness of it all. This really is the bottom line. The front line. I have no control on this battlefield of random malfunction. All I can do is wait for the bell. When it eventually goes and everyone races out of the classroom, Liam is the last to leave. He looks downtrodden, tired.

'Bye Liam.'
'Bye Sir.'
'Oh and Liam, forget about the C3…'
'What do you mean, Sir?'
'The C3, it never happened.'
'Thank you, Sir.'
'One more thing…'
'Yes Sir?'
'Stop stealing pencils.'
'Ok Sir.'

A GAME OF CONSEQUENCES

The Reward and Consequences system introduced into secondary schools in 2010 goes down very well with students. Two separate charts are displayed on the wall of every classroom, clearly for all to see and observe. The kids know these charts off by heart, in particular the Consequences one. Herein lies, in great detail, a fully navigateable selection of punishments in ascending order of severity. So you can work out what you can get away with and when. It's a new currency with which to live your life during lessons. Of course, some C's are more easily denied or fought against than others and if you're not clever about it you'll lose the game. But that's the point, it's like a game, and the students have all the cards.

One person telling a lot of other people what to do has always been a bit of an issue. People don't like being told what to do, especially when they are young. Most office workers adhere to a stringent set of time-keeping rules, which is why people feel a sense of gratification when they get away with breaking them, like going home early for instance, especially if what they are doing is a bit boring. People like going out to play, just like children do. Adults get told off all the time. People look at the clock when someone's late for work in the morning and make funny remarks:

'Afternoon Dave…'

Or if someone comes back 10 minutes late from lunch:

SPIKE WEBB

'Nice of you to join us this afternoon...'

When people go off sick for a couple of days they have to make sure they don't go anywhere near where they work in case they get seen:

'I saw Helen coming out of the hairdresser's yesterday and she looked the picture of health – I thought she was supposed to have the flu!'

So controlling people who don't want to be controlled is a bit of a game. But what's the one thing you don't do at the start of any game? Put all your cards on the table, face up for all to see. And that's exactly what this Consequences chart has done. It enables kids to navigate the punishment system to suit themselves.

Here's a typical example:

Naughty Martin has been told that if he carries on pushing Connor's chair and making a noise while Miss is talking he'll get a C1. He knows what a C1 is, it's just a warning, and he hasn't got it yet. So when Miss isn't looking he kicks Connor's chair again because, after all, it is really funny and it makes other people laugh. So Miss plays her next card:

'Right Martin, that's a C1.'

But Martin has another card up his sleeve:

'Ahh Miss, it wasn't me this time, it was Connor!'

It's a nice try, but Miss is sticking to her guns:

'C1 warning Martin, next time it'll be a C2.'

The thing is, Martin had already figured he could afford a C1, most kids can as it's only a warning. But a C2? He'll calm it down a bit but if things get really fun with Connor and the others are lovin' it then he'll go for a C2 as well. He'll probably stop short of a C3 though 'cos that's a detention after school and he's got footy tonight.

The fact is, list all your students' disciplinary options on the wall at the start of every lesson and they will turn them to their advantage. Display all your cards before the game even starts and they will walk all over you.

For the kids, it's game on.

For the teachers, it's game over.

TAKE COVER!

* * *

Moreover, displaying a consequences chart on the wall of the classroom is an open admission that previous attempts to administer discipline in modern schools and academies have completely failed.

So full marks for transparency in local education, although this system appears to be the most damaging disciplinary device to be introduced so far. When I was at school (quite a long time ago) discipline seemed to operate comfortably under the assumption that students would obey their teachers with an understanding that punishments would be administered in instances where there is deviation from the established norm. The Consequences system effectively announces the complete opposite, setting a precedent that of course students are expected to misbehave, because that is an established state of affairs that we have to accept.

The message used to be:

'We expect you to behave. if you do not, there will be consequences.'

Now the message is:

'We expect you to misbehave, so here are the consequences.'

It is tantamount to saying to the students:

'We admit we couldn't really control you properly, and as you know, we're not allowed to use physical force or language that might offend you or hurt your feelings in any way, and of course, you know your rights as a human being, so here's a chart showing what might sometimes happen when you misbehave.'

Nice one. As a cocky student that would suit me down to the ground. I've got a list of all the stuff I may or may not want to do, complete with codes of severity telling me what will happen if and when I decide to take part in this new game. And the best news of all?

I'm in control!

These new methods have completely eradicated any sense of fear or mystery. If you know exactly what might or might not happen to you, there is no sense of the unknown to provide a no-go area. Ok, you might not like the idea of staying behind after school in detention for a C3, and you could be a little nervous or perplexed at the idea of teachers phoning your parents to tell on you if you get a C4, or even having a meeting with your form teacher and your mum and dad to discuss your behaviour issues after a C5. But none of this is very scary is it?

The most commonly used disciplinary threat is a C3, and you will get one of these for various offenses which constitute refusing to knuckle down, preferring to mess around instead. If you are bestowed with one of these, it means that you must stay behind after school from 3.15 until 4pm, during which time you can mess about some more. Or, if the teacher responsible for supervising after school C3 duties is particularly stern, you can use the time to get some homework out of the way so you can carry on messing about at home.

Of course, if you really don't want to turn up for your C3, you can always get your mum to ring up and say you've got a dental appointment, or even take issue with the C3 itself, which could mean a meeting with the school at some point. If you refuse to turn up to C3's they simply stack up, so you owe the school stay-behind time, a bit like a debt or overdraft. This results in further disciplinary measures and more meetings with parents and teachers, possible C4's C5's and all the rest of it. If you get this far, there's little chance of going back to a fresh start so there's not much point in bothering.

In reality, the consequence of rigorous and meticulous use of the consequences chart is that, in a particularly unruly class, there will be very few people actually left in the room. You can be sent out into an 'exit room' for simply refusing to do as you are told. Or swearing. So teachers must use the threat of consequences a bit sparingly. And students know this, which makes the game even easier for them to play and win. Ultimately, in a school where messing about is a particularly high priority amongst its students, administering the correct consequences wherever appropriate would result in a building awash with students in endless meetings with teachers and

TAKE COVER!

parents or sitting in exclusion rooms and all the classrooms would be virtually empty.

Call me old-fashioned, but I believe that every school or academy should have a door along one of the corridors which is rarely opened, behind which resides a man who everyone is afraid of, students and teachers alike. The teachers are afraid because the buck stops with him, and the students are afraid because he is where the real trouble starts. This man is called a head master, and he is rarely seen during school hours. And if you do see him, you had better do your tie up and walk quietly by in an orderly manner.

However, a head master (or head teacher as we must refer to them these days) will never inspire that sense of awe if he insists on standing at the school gates every morning and evening, shaking hands with colleagues and parents and having a laugh with the students.

There will be some civil servants and bureaucrats in the government's education department who will not agree. And, if they ever get to read this, they may even be a bit cross. But I'm a grown-up and entitled to articulate my opinion. There's no 'C' for that.

But there may be consequences.

GOING OVER THE TOP

I'm off to cover a geography lesson at another school I occasionally get sent to, St Christopher Academy. It's Thursday morning, period 3, another double so 80 minutes long, and I'm tired. What's more, it's year 9 (14-year-olds) who can be the most difficult to control. Still, it's a slightly nicer school where the kids aren't quite so tough and the behaviour seems a good deal better, so it won't be too bad.

I walk past the year 9 students as they line up in the corridor outside the classroom door. They are fresh-faced, cheeky and irritatingly chirpy. Some of the boys are taller than me, and one is built like a rugby player. I walk past quickly, smiling politely to show I'm 'one of them' and make for the teacher's desk to look for the cover work.

They storm into the classroom and position themselves for battle. I wait until they are all seated and address them using my contrived I'm confident, in control but also a good bloke really countenance:

'Good afternoon. My name is Mr Webb.'

'Good afternoon, Sir!'

'This is the volume at which I speak, I expect everything else to be lower than this for the next hour and twenty minutes – do we have a deal?'

'Yes Sir.'

TAKE COVER!

'Pages 137 to 139 in your Geography text books, complete exercises 2 and 3. When that's done, I'll hand out some work sheets with a land graph exercise for you to complete.'

Already several boys are huddling and discussing their school football team's next scheduled game, which is just a few days away. They are talking about who is to play in what position etc. The conversation is for the benefit of everyone present, as the whole class is keen for them to do well. Even the girls are joining in, as befits the current tendency for many robust and modern-minded women to take a keen interest in the sport.

Trouble is, this isn't sport, it's geography. And as a Cover Support Teacher I am charged with the task of changing the subject. I must persuade these young adults that for the next hour it will be more beneficial and potentially quite interesting to concentrate on methods of localised land irrigation and the effects of artificial water management on the environment instead of the use of natural land formations and resources, and of course the subsequent economic ramifications of the deployment of one as opposed to the other.

Of course, I don't actually know anything about this. I just have to tell them that reading about it in their text books and writing about it in their exercise books is preferable to talking about a football game; their football game, which is to take place soon and will then be over. The land irrigation stuff will still be there next week. It'll probably still be there when these people have finished school, been to college or worked for their Dads, taken a year out to travel, got themselves a trade, got themselves some kids, worked, got made redundant, worked again and then retired.

The fact is, football is exciting and irrigation isn't. But I have a job to do:

'Come on everyone, pages 137 to 139 in your text books.'

They look at me briefly before continuing with their conversations. As a kind of token gesture, they pick up their text books and some even open them at the correct pages and actually begin to work. I press them a little further:

SPIKE WEBB

'Come on, I know it's not as interesting as football, but you're here to study geography for the next hour and a bit, so let me see you getting some answers down on paper.'

They quieten down and although there is still some murmuring and random kicking under the desks, things settle nicely down as I pace around the room. For the next hour (I'm always glancing at the clock), I am periodically engaged in the suppression of missile throwing, pens and screwed up pieces of paper occasionally taking to the air and people asking to go to the toilet. But it's all do-able. Calm even.

But it is the calm before the storm.

I notice a piece of paper is being passed around between the footballers. I decide to wait until I know what is on the paper before addressing the situation. Soon an opportunity arises for me to find out, as I look over the shoulder of someone who has opened it out behind the cover of his upturned geography text book. It is an aerial diagram of a football pitch with names of players in their various positions, plus some suggested corrections and alternatives that have been added during the course of its journey around the room.

It's a game plan. It's also part of a game I don't really want to play. Because I'm tired. Tired of pacing around, looking at the clock, intercepting flying objects. Tired of wondering if I'll get through this last 20 minutes without too much added stress. It's a game and I don't want to play.

So I decide to ignore it. I simply walk past as if I haven't noticed. But the game plan has served its purpose because soon the conversation about the football begins again. At first, it's an animated murmur but soon grows into excited banter. The noise levels rise almost uncontrollably as I glance through the window in the classroom door and spy the teacher in the room opposite, speaking to his class in complete control. But in here, it's more like a lively pub.

It's game on, and I don't want to play.

I try to look philosophical as I raise my voice:

'Thank you everyone, that's enough!'

They are almost shouting now.

'I said that's enough!'

TAKE COVER!

Then they bring out a weapon I didn't know they had. Staring excitedly at me, they begin to emit a classic, low choral note in unison. It's one of those techniques that teams of sportsmen and even some rock bands use to gee themselves up before a striking performance. It starts off low and gradually builds to a loud climax.

I'm almost transfixed as this ever-increasing wave of noise races towards me, building in strength like a tsunami of sound, eventually reaching a deafening crescendo accompanied by fists banging on tables. I stare at this pack of baying wolves in disbelief. I'm like a rabbit in the headlights. This is a full-on attack on every mortal fibre that contains the concept of authority. But that's not all.

It's personal. It's an attack on me. Somewhere along the line they have detected a weak spot, my Achilles heel. Maybe I smiled or grinned in sympathy at something, or simply looked a bit tired. But somehow, they saw their chance, their opportunity to go the whole way, firing on all guns. One girl is looking at me with a concerned, sympathetic smile, almost worried for me, as if observing someone who has just flopped miserably at a talent contest, bombed on their first attempt at stand-up comedy or an actor who's lost his nerve on his opening night. And her face makes it even worse, because I wanted them to respect me. I wanted them to like me. Instead, they are laughing at me. They are making as much noise as is humanly possible to do in a classroom. They have triumphed in this war of authority versus complete defiance. And they are loving every moment.

They are in heaven.

And I am in hell.

I don't know what to do. I look at them quizzically, but inside I am consumed with anger, furious because I wanted them to like me. Furious because I wanted this little job to work, for a short while at least. Furious because I have to be here at all.

Still they roar.

And I'm furious because I'm struggling to pay the Virgin Broadband bill and this month's credit card payment.

SPIKE WEBB

Furious because I no longer have a nice exciting job in advertising up in London that pays really well. Furious because I can't ring my wife on a Friday afternoon and say 'fancy a curry tonight love?'

And I'm furious because I still haven't got anywhere with all those dreams and schemes I've been having since I got made redundant years ago. Furious because I didn't accept my university place and get a degree that would guarantee me a good job for life.

Still they roar.

And I'm furious because I can't pop into my Mum's on the way home and tell her all about it. She was a teacher – a proper one. Furious because she died three years ago and I still can't believe she's gone. Furious because although I believe in God, I still don't know if nice things are really in store for us when we die.

And furious because my feet still hurt in these crap shoes.

Still they roar.

And just as I thought I was getting the hang of this cover teaching business, this happens. Yes, I'm very cross indeed.

But there's no point in trying to yell at them as I wouldn't have a chance of being heard. So I decide to go lateral. I stroll calmly to the door of the classroom and slowly open it, staring vacantly at the baying mob. Their voices subside. They haven't the faintest idea what I'm going to do, and neither have I. Inside I am seething with rage, but outwardly in complete control.

I speak to them calmly, but with force:
'Who is it to be then?'
'What?'
'Who is going there?'
'Where Sir?'
'To see the head guy of course!'
'What, the head teacher?'
'Yes, absolutely.'
I start pointing at the main ring leaders at random.

TAKE COVER!

'Could it be you... or you... or maybe you?'

They are looking worried now.

'I am in the process of making my decision with regard to who is to seek the company of the head teacher. In the meantime, the remainder of this lesson will be conducted in complete...'

And I bellow with all the strength of voice I can muster:

'SILENCE!!!'

They gasp, then I slam the door shut so hard it makes the room shudder. All is completely quiet. Smiling almost sadistically, I ask calmly:

'Do I make myself completely clear?'

'Yes, Sir.'

The class look down, some stifling nervous giggles as I begin to pace up and down at the front with my hands behind my back, making every pace loud and menacingly audible – a bit like a German commandant in World War Two. As I do this, there is complete silence for the final ten minutes of the lesson, marred only by the odd cheeky noise accompanied by more stifled giggling. But that's just random shrapnel to me. I've won the battle. I've won, and I've discovered a new skill.

I have become an actor.

NO MAN'S LAND

I'm standing on the stairs, half way up a stairwell between floors in the English block. I have deliberately positioned myself about midway up and although stationary, I have adopted the pose of one who is in transit. If you were to take a photograph of me as I climb the stairs, this would be the result.

Why have I done this?

Because I'm hiding. Hiding from the head teacher. And also the English department, where I'm supposed to be working. Put simply, I want the head teacher to think that I am in an English lesson somewhere and I want people from the English department to think that I'm in the staff room. However, in the unfortunate event of any of these people using the staircase for whatever reason, I don't want them to catch me here just standing around with nothing to do. That is why I have assumed the countenance of one who is busily on his way somewhere, so that if anyone else appears I can simply continue purposefully up the stairs.

This is Ashfields, the second school I've been sent to on a regular basis for some weeks now. Although set in the middle of a particularly rough estate, It's quite a nice school. Smaller than my first one with tougher students, but nonetheless it has a nice feel about it. I've been cover support for a range of lessons, but recently it has been suggested that I take up a more focused role, providing extra English tuition on basic grammar to smaller classes on a regular basis. This is something I have been keen to take up, flattered that they

TAKE COVER!

should want me to do it at all. After all, I'm not a qualified secondary school teacher, so it's good to know they think I'm up to it.

My forthcoming increased involvement in the English Department has meant that I am called in to the school on some days even though there is little or no cover work. Sometimes, on request, I spend time at the back of an English lesson to get to know some of the students, their abilities and behavior patterns and also to experience at first hand the teaching styles and methods of the teachers themselves, which are, without exception highly impressive, especially given the endless challenges presented to them by teenagers with considerable behavioral problems. And when I'm not providing cover or standing at the back of a classroom observing, the intention is for me to occupy a desk in a small exit room on the second floor of the English block, using a computer to familiarise myself with certain learning objectives and initial skills assessment tests. So I have a kind of office to reside in when I'm not actually in a classroom.

But now there is a problem. I have spent enough observation time in English lessons and not wanting to overstay my welcome in fellow teacher's classrooms, my natural habitat when not providing cover is my little office. However, this is now almost always occupied by teacher assistants providing extra one-to-one tuition to backward students, where they cannot be interrupted.

So the only place left to go when I'm not working is the staff room in the central school block, where I can sit and drink coffee, which is nice. The trouble with this is the staff room is inconveniently located opposite the head teacher's office and is also a connecting room to other important parts of the school, like the library and alternative corridors leading to other department blocks and classrooms. So there's a lot of through traffic. The place is quite the hub of activity, even during lesson time. The head teacher pops in quite a bit, as do other members of staff including the head of Cover Support whose responsibilities include making sure people like me have plenty of work to do. Recently I have become aware that I am spending far too much time in the staff room and I've been questioned on more than one occasion about how it's all going and how busy they're keeping me. So, not wanting to draw any more attention to myself, I've taken to roaming the corridors and loitering in nooks and crannies around the school in my old overcoat, which isn't ideal either.

So I've come up with the ideal solution. I select a place where I could be legitimately going about my business, adopt an appropriate stance, and freeze myself in time. If I hear footsteps approach, or if someone by chance enters the vicinity, I resume my apparent journey. I continue to the top of the stairs, through some double doors, onto the second-floor landing, through another set of doors and then down the opposite stairwell, where I become static again, this time facing downward. When the bell goes and people come rushing onto the stairs, I simply continue my journey to an appropriate place; either to a classroom if I have cover duties, the staff room if it's break time or another stairwell where I become frozen in time once more. Occasionally, on my way from one spot to another, I may engage in brief banter with other friendly members of staff:

'On the move again I see! All go isn't it?'

'Yep, lots on today...'

True, it's a bit of a lonely existence. In fact, it's difficult to decide what feels more lonely: pacing up and down in a classroom of teenagers, most of whom don't want to be there, or posing rigidly still on a staircase? But I can't afford to turn down work and it looks as though I'm going to end up with some regular, real teaching work.

So here I am at my usual post in the stairwell. I have earlier taken a cover lesson in maths before grabbing a quick coffee in the staff room at break time. I have no more cover work until this afternoon in the PE block, my little office is occupied and the Head Teacher and the Head of Cover Supply are still in the staff room, so I have had no option but to take up my usual position half way up the staircase, waiting for the bell to go. My mind wanders a little. What on earth am I doing? I'm 57 years old and I'm at school playing statues, stuck on a

TAKE COVER!

staircase hiding from my head teacher! I'm so engrossed in this irony that I fail to notice someone at the foot of the stairwell looking up at me through the gaps in the steps. It's one of the teachers whose classes I've been observing:

'Something keeping you, Sir? You almost look poised for a military assault!'

I spring into action and move hastily up the remaining steps with a fumbled reply:

'Can't quite remember where I'm supposed to be…'

Nice one. A Cover Support Supply Teacher who's stuck half way up a school staircase and doesn't appear to know where he is or where he is going. Embarrassed to say the least, something tells me my expertise at real-life freeze framing may have backfired.

As it turns out, today is to be my last day at this school. The teaching agency calls me on my way home. Apparently the head teacher has contacted them saying he feels they really need a full-time GCSE professional to take up my intended position – so it's all off as far as I'm concerned. Of course, that could mean anything. It might be something to do with slashed budgets not facilitating extra curriculum specialist tuition, or maybe the parents aren't keen on the idea.

But being caught playing truant on the stairs certainly won't have helped.

PURE COWARDICE

I'm back in the toilets again, hiding. But this time I really am hiding, not from the usual stuff like my uncertainties, insecurities etc, but another person. A real person. Last night, in the corridor just outside the cleaner's cupboard in the Ladies toilets, I was approached by Eva, a Swedish cleaner who finds it difficult to speak English at the best of times, let alone when she is asking awkward questions.

Eva, like me, is a cleaner and part of our little team. Along with a couple of others, she cleans the office tables and empties the waste paper bins. I clean the toilets and floors. Eva is particularly close to our supervisor, a likeable Watford cockney called Fizz, and they like to go outside and smoke together. I don't have a problem with that because I don't come here to smoke, I come here to clean. But Eva seems to have adopted Fizz as her special cleaning friend, her confidante even. Not just her supervisor.

So yesterday, I am approached by Eva who I gather, after some deciphering, wants me to give her five pounds towards a birthday present for our illustrious leader and cleaning supervisor Fizz, whose birthday it is next week. I fumbled about in my pockets and, of course, pleading temporary poverty, mumbled something about sorting something out the next day. My problem is that the principle reason I come to this place and clean up other people's mess is to get some money. And as ever with this kind of activity, it's not much money. It amounts to £15 a night (£7.50 an hour),

TAKE COVER!

which is paid monthly in arrears. And as such, £5 is a substantial part of a night's work. And at the moment, I don't have a spare fiver to give to someone I hardly know, and certainly not well enough to smoke with.

If I wasn't in real need of money, I wouldn't be here. I'd hardly be dropping by anyway to hang out with a gang of cleaners as part of my social life with the added benefit of a bit of cash on the side, and frankly neither would Fizz. But it seems to be the intention of the very sweet and caring Eva to present Fizz with a lavish birthday gift on behalf of herself and her cleaning comrades.

However, rather than attempt to explain my position on this to someone who finds it hard to understand even basic English, and also because I'm too embarrassed to admit to that degree of miserly scroogism, I have decided to revert to my usual pastime, hiding.

I can hear Eva in the cleaning closet cupboard and I know she's on the warpath. Earlier she burst into the corridor towards the mens' with a searching and determined look on her face. She didn't see me and I quickly selected trap 2 in the Ladies and locked myself in.

So here I am, a 57-year-old man hiding in a toilet cubicle from a mad Swedish woman who wants my money. And that's twice in one day I've been hiding. I really should go into some sort of espionage.

One thing's for sure, the pay would be better.

DOG FIGHT

It's period 4 on a Friday morning and I'm in one of the computer rooms at Gatesbury School. I'm in charge of a class of sixteen-year-olds who are revising for their imminent GCSE exam in Travel and Tourism. They have chosen this course over other options as it's more interesting, offering a more comprehensive range of topics and study areas that are particularly relevant to modern day living, especially for young people with a penchant for travel and any opportunities that may arise enabling them to see more of the world.

So why have three young men decided to marvel and giggle at the snarling faces of viscous dogs on the internet instead? Standing at my vantage point at the front desk (I always stand) I can see dozens of vile, salivating beasts displayed on their computer screens, which are affording these students a good deal of joy and stifled laughter. I try and imagine circumstances under which snarling dogs could somehow be included in the study of Travel and Tourism. Perhaps they feature in an area of the course that deals with things to be avoided when visiting key cities of the world? Or are these images to be used as visual metaphors for common dangers that must be observed when travelling to foreign countries?

I think not. I decide to start strolling round the room in my usual fashion, to assert my position as Cover Teacher. I move slowly at first so as to give the three dog watchers time to refresh their screens to something more resembling course

TAKE COVER!

work. The first two do this with consummate ease, but the third in line is so engrossed with these foul images that his dogs are still on screen as I pass alongside. I feel obliged to comment:

'I assume these dogs are part of your Travel and Tourism course?'

'Oh yes Sir, something we covered a while back.'

Nevertheless, he quickly refreshes his screen and a majestic picture of New York's Central Park appears in all its glory. That is to indicate that our conversation is over because we both know that those dogs have nothing whatsoever to do with the intricacies of modern day travel. Of course, if I pursue the issue he could argue that Central Park is well known for its many dangerous wild dogs that must be avoided at all costs and that this is merely a necessary box to tick as part of the study area. Technically, I am not in a position to contradict him as I have never studied the subject, so I'm more than happy to leave it at that and continue on my way around the room.

I move slowly to the other side of the room, observing pictures of capital cities, airports and pages from all kinds of online travel information sites and most students seem to be concentrating on their course work revision. Some images put this slightly in question, like fancy looking mobile phones accompanied by knocked down prices, but hey, who am I to question these? Everyone needs a mobile phone to stay in one place these days, let alone go anywhere else, so they must surely feature in Travel and Tourism right?

Anyway, somewhat unsurprisingly, the sound of laughter resumes back at the other side of the room. I am acutely aware that the dogs have probably returned to the three screens over yonder as the pitch and audible texture of the stifled laughter is exactly the same as before, so it follows that the subject matter must be the same also. The only difference is an increase in intensity which is verging on the hysterical. They have clearly stumbled upon some even more ferocious canine monstrosities. Of course, I could dash back round, catch them before they refresh their screens to delightful visuals of New York, Paris, Rome and the like shouting 'No dogs allowed!' and deliver a tirade on the importance of revision in preparation for GCSEs, but what would be the point? This particular period of time is not going to make any difference to their exam performance, especially given that, as near grown-ups, they appear to have decided that it's not necessary. And why do I need to concern myself with the forthcoming exam results of three complete strangers when I'm being paid a fraction more than I am as an office cleaner in the evenings? Frankly, I'd rather clean the classroom.

But part of me does care. Partly because I have a job to do and I don't like not doing things properly, especially when I'm being paid, however little that is. So I make my way back round to the dog watchers and sure enough, when I approach, I see nothing but images of some of the world's most beautiful cities plus some sample flight booking options and general Travel and Tourism stuff. This ritual continues for most of the rest of the lesson.

Just before the end, I take a final turn around the room to see that my dog watchers have tired of the canine horrors. They are now amusing themselves with pictures of horribly contorted human faces, the features of which are either the product of some intricate and skilled photoshop work, or simply belong to some seriously unfortunate human beings who have been furnished with considerably less than their fair share of what is generally considered to be normal looks. Then, just as I'm wondering why these contorted faces, dogs and men alike, should be the cause of such joy and mirth, the bell goes and it's the end of Travel and Tourism.

Ah well, it takes all sorts.

UNARMED COMBAT

I'm in a science room waiting for a class of year tens at Gatesbury. On my cover register there are only 10 names, which experience has taught me is not particularly good news. It can signify that the class has been kept small because they are difficult to handle. To make matters worse, being a science room, they will be sitting on high stools facing me at long benches, ready for action. And when some of them decide to get up and walk around, which is inevitable, they will be in close vicinity to sinks and taps which can be turned off and on, which can be fun when you're bored and want to express yourself. It also means they have unlimited access to water and endless opportunities to fill their water bottles, which they are allowed to have by law. It is against the Human Rights Act to prevent a person taking sips of water from a plastic bottle on a regular basis, and this is especially important if that person happens to be incarcerated in a classroom. Of course, students must keep their pledge to drink responsibly and use the water merely to sustain their existence in the context of life support, for which it is intended.

But at the end of the day, water can be such fun.

So I'm not much looking forward to the next hour. Soon I hear the approach and there is already a good deal of unruly noise. As they saunter in, my heart sinks still further as I recognise the violent, fist bashing 15-year-old called Jack from the multiplagons class a while back. This bunch are accompanied by a Teacher's Assistant whom I recognize from the staff room, so at least I'm going to have some help in here. I deliver my usual spiel about noise levels and take the register. The class have positioned themselves next to their favourite partners in crime at the two benches in front of me, with the exception of Jack who has chosen to sit on top of the work bench that runs along the back of the room in front of an open window, dangling and swinging his legs back and forth in the manner of one who intends to relax and unwind for an hour or so. He has his water bottle at the ready and occasionally takes dramatically long gulps, with the bottle raised almost vertically upwards toward the ceiling to emphasise the pure joy of thirst quenching when doubled up as an act of defiance. I imagine him gesturing in a similar way in the near future with a bottle of lager outside a pub somewhere. I remember that he has a 5-minute time-out option that can be brought into play if things get a little too difficult for him, or indeed any teacher, teacher support or cover support supply person.

So that's good to know. I decide to ignore Jack's clear statement of intentions and give out the work, which has been left on the teacher's front bench. These teenagers are required to create a poster which is to be used as a revision map, outlining the key features of one of the elements of science they have been studying. I write these on the board: A large tray of coloured pens and pencils has been left on the front bench, and much ado is made of selecting these, not unlike that which occurs when people throw bits of bread among pigeons in the high street. But at least it shows that they are keen to do something. I am pleased to see that all of them, including Jack who has now sat down on his own at the far end of the bench, are starting to design their posters.

So I start walking around, looking over shoulders at the developing posters and giving encouragement.

'That looks good', 'Coming along nicely', 'looking forward to seeing how that one turns out!'

Even Jack has started something quite colourful to do with friction. I decide to make the most of this positive development:

'That looks great Jack, well done...'

TAKE COVER!

However, before long there's the usual fracas from a bunch of boys who have already become bored with the poster. A playful scuffle results in a poster falling to the floor. This instigates an immediate response from its owner and another one ends up on the floor. I move over to calm it down. My problem is that if I pick up the posters and put them back on the bench, I am occupying a position of subservience, which is dangerous, because thereafter these kids will see that as a green light to do what they want. However, they kind of have that anyway as the only weapons I have are Consequences, and they probably couldn't care less about those. But on the other hand, if I insist that someone retrieves the posters, that will begin a new argument as to who started the whole poster throwing business. And even if that does get resolved, the boy selected to pick up the poster will make the most of climbing down from the stool, crawling around under the bench, where he will be kicked by the others, or strolling round the bench to pick them up, pushing and shoving his comrades as he goes, which in turn will cause more incidents.

I decide upon the easier option. After all, it's mid afternoon and I'm knackered. With an inward sigh, I pick up the posters and remonstrate:

'Come on gentlemen, enough of that. I want to see some great posters...'

Then there's a commotion over at the far end of the room. A cheeky girl called Ellie and two friends have opened what is an alternative exit onto a grass area opposite the school football pitches. They are gesturing and giggling at some other kids, mainly boys, who are watching an outdoor PE lesson. Luckily, the teaching assistant is onto it straight away and goes over to them. She knows these teenagers much better than I do and can address them as individuals by name, which helps. She manages to get them away from the door, but on closing it there is much remonstration:

'Leave it open Miss – it's hot in here.'

The assistant is very good at what she does, but her efforts are equally impaired by the lack of disciplinary tools at her disposal. The lesson continues in much the same way, with pockets of incidents occurring one after the other, some posters become paper airplanes and it's almost impossible to keep Ellie and her gang seated. They have taken to playing with the taps, splashing water at each other, filling water bottles as elaborately as possible and squealing with laughter. At one point I lose it with Ellie:

'Right, that's enough Ellie, outside in the corridor!'
'No! I'm not going out there…'
'It's either that or sit down!'

Defiantly, she flicks her head back but moves back to her place with her friends, deliberately slowly in an effort to antagonize even more. Instead of recommencing their poster designs though, they produce their mobile phones and huddle up for some fun Youtube viewing:

'Mobile phones away please!'
'In a minute Sir!'

But then something happens to distract my attention. The TA is trying to reason with Jack, who, having by now become bored of his poster, has taken possession of a large, plastic foam-filled dice (What on earth is that doing in here anyway?) and is kicking it around the room. It's about the size of a small football. What is also worrying is that he is clearly enjoying the release of pent up aggression as he aims the ball at various objects in the room. I'm aware that this has to be stopped or what's left of the lesson will descend into a complete free-for-all. So I move over.

'Come on, give me the dice.'
'No!'
'You can't play with that in here – you need to be getting on with your poster.'
'Bored with that.'
'But it was good…'
'Don't care.'

I reach to take the dice from him, aware that it is illegal to actually touch him, which he knows only too well. A look of slight amusement appears on his face as he raises the dice out of my reach.

'It'll be a C3…'

TAKE COVER!

'Don't care.'

As I move to take the dice again he throws it over towards my teacher's bench. I turn to see that Ellie has left her seat and is now standing there, poised to catch the dice, which she does. Cue rapturous applause from the rest of the class.

I move over towards Ellie, who throws the dice back to jack, who, approaching, catches it and throws it back to Ellie. Soon I'm stuck in the middle, trying desperately to catch the plastic dice as they throw it to each other. In fact, I've inadvertently joined in the game and become piggy in the middle. And as you'd expect, others begin to join in too. Everyone, with the exception of the TA who is as exasperated as I am, finds this highly amusing and show their appreciation accordingly with much yelping and clapping of hands.

And it is laughable, because here is a Cover Support Teacher, apparently in a position of authority, who instead of presiding over the studious construction of scientific revision posters, is playing piggy in the middle in a science laboratory with a load of teenagers and a plastic dice. We might as well be out on that playing field.

Eventually I manage to catch the ball, to which there is a low rumble of anticipation from the class. Jack approaches:

'Give it back!'

'No, sit down.'

'Sir says I can have it as long as I don't break it.'

'Eh?'

'Like a stress ball!'

In a flash, he whips the dice out of my hand. He is now facing me, daring me to do something. He is challenging me, and somehow, I must respond. I could attempt to wrestle the dice out of his hand without touching his person, but instead, I snatch it quickly back and walk away. But Jack's not having any of it. He follows me back to the front bench:

'Give it back!'

I turn to face him.

He looks determined and this may result in him attempting to take the dice using physical force, which would be assault on his part (a C6, incidentally) but I'm thinking he doesn't really care about much at all, let alone consequences of any kind. So unless I do some quick, decisive thinking, I'm in a very difficult position indeed. Standing in front of me, Jack is about my height as I am shorter than average. He's quite stocky for a 15-year-old, and probably quite strong. And here's the thing, he's very worked up and doesn't seem to care who he upsets. But being a drummer, I'm strong too. I'm not sure which of us would win in a fight. Of course, entering into unarmed combat is completely out of the question. But he looks about to take the dice back using force. The whole class are watching to see what happens. There's ten minutes to go so I'm not going to be saved by the bell. Of course, I could start another game by throwing it to someone else and end this delightful afternoon with another game of good old piggy in the middle, but it's not exactly supervision at its best is it? It might even get back to the staff room via the TA, which would be embarrassing to say the least.

To my relief, the TA intervenes by suggesting that Jack takes his 5-minute time-out option. Jack agrees to this, providing he can take the dice with him, which I agree to because frankly I never want to see it again and there's only 10 minutes to go anyway.

Jack thus dealt with, I turn back into the classroom to see that Ellie and her pals are sitting in the open doorway in the sunshine having a good old natter. As I approach, I can hear that they are discussing the intricacies of a forthcoming party event at the weekend, with particular emphasis on who is to attend and who will definitely not be welcome. There is absolutely no point in my attempting to re-introduce the scientific posters into the mix at this stage, so I begin to gather up those that have been attempted. There are some at least, which I suppose is something. Then comes the sound of the bell, which can sometimes be unnerving when it announces another treck into the unknown, but on this occasion is a blissful sound, heralding as it does the onset of blessed release.

So, to recap, a boy called Jack, who admittedly has some serious behavioral issues, goes to a science lesson, draws a couple of pictures on a piece of paper, gets bored and makes it

TAKE COVER!

into a paper airplane. Then he embarks on an amusing game involving a plastic dice. And after all the fun has died down, he can chill out in the corridor for a while and get his breath back. If he smoked, he could even spark up a fag and chill some more.

He's got rights, after all.

* * *

On the way home, sinking back into the seat in my usual spot at the back of the bus, I'm musing over my day as usual. And as ever, it's a bit of a blur. But what is clearer than day is the precarious position I was in back in that science lab. I was glad of the presence of the Teaching Assistant who was a great help. But on the other hand, it can't have done my reputation any good to be in such an embarrassing and potentially explosive situation. Then again, it probably happens all the time and they're simply happy to have someone prepared to stick it in there for an hour.

But what if that kid had actually started pushing and shoving to get that dice back? Forbidden as I am to even exercise physical restraint, I would have had to back away and send the TA to fetch assistance from SLT (School Leadership Team). When I was at school, on the rare occasions when someone needed to be seriously dealt with, the teacher was perfectly within his or her rights to use reasonable force to eject that person from the room. I must have seen this happen twice in seven years in secondary school, and the incident would be talked about for days after. The point is, it's surely fairer to the kids themselves to present them with a physical ultimatum that is guaranteed to put an end to their confused response to being able to do exactly what they want. Is being removed from a room by force really a traumatising experience? Rather that it firmly demonstrates that there are boundaries to be observed which create a much-needed level of security. At the end of the day, these people are not adults. And what about the human rights of the teachers traumatised by unacceptable behavior that is seemingly unchallengeable, except with the use of a

SPIKE WEBB

Consequences chart which is nothing more than a half-baked attempt to appeal to a kid's better sense of reason, but in reality plays host to their greater sense of manipulation and childish skullduggery.

Of course, no-one wants to end up actually fighting. Imagine the job spec:

'Must be educated to degree level and have some teacher training experience. A good, natural rapport with young teenagers is a must in this environment. The successful applicant should also be fairly handy with their fists. A level 3 or equivalent in bare knuckle boxing, taekwondo or kick boxing would be an advantage, although full training will be given.'

And at the end of the day, I'm paid 70 quid for roughly a 7-hour day. So that's £10 an hour, and as I've mentioned before, that's slightly more than I get as a cleaner. And If there's ever any bloodshed, I'd rather clean it up than be the man responsible for it.

EERIE SILENCE

Complete silence in a classroom, rare though that is, can be a problem. It can completely challenge your view of yourself, particularly if you're not a proper teacher. On this occasion, I have achieved this quietude with the help of another – a real teacher, in fact. At the beginning of this cover support lesson, I have given out task sheets which the class's usual science teacher has set in the form of a test. Most classes will ignore this ploy as simply a way of keeping them quiet in teacher's absence. And they'd be right, it's simply an attempt to make life easier for the likes of me and more importantly themselves, as they can always use it again another time.

However, this class seem to be taking it seriously.

'Is this a real test Sir?'

'Will it be marked?'

Naturally I've seized the opportunity to guarantee myself an easy hour-long stroll around the classroom as they scribble in earnest and affirmed their worst fears that it is indeed a test which will be duly marked and assessed. And they believed me, which is unusual.

So here I am, pacing up and down, happy at this rare but peaceful outcome. But something makes me feel uncomfortable. I am acutely aware of my position of authority over these 30 or so individuals, something I spend most of my time desperately trying to establish. But now I've got it, I feel like an imposter, because I know that five will get you ten this test will not be marked and they really have nothing to worry about. I can feel their restlessness and part of me hates the futility of it – it's not as though they are doing it because they want to learn, they've just been conned again, successfully this time. But still I am compelled to force the silence.

After about 30 minutes, people are beginning to snigger and make daft noises every now and then. The collective attention span is clearly wavering a bit. Maybe they've started to realise that, with a few exceptions, teachers rarely care much about what happens during cover periods. Still, it's only the occasional snigger with a bit of nudging.

There's a big guy in the middle of the class who's inclined to take this the furthest. Or maybe he's just more noticeable because he's significantly taller and stockier than everyone else. His grin is also broader. I could force him to sit at the front on his own below my raised front teacher's desk in silence, but I know I will hate doing that. I'll feel sorry for him. I shouldn't, but I will, because it's a human thing. I don't want to make another human being feel awful in front of everyone else for 30 minutes until the end of the period. Of course, it would do him good if the punishment was just, but it isn't, and he'll have a big sense of injustice if I single him out. He will feel bitter at being selected as an example simply because he's more noticeable. He will feel wrongly victimised. And the memories of instances like that can stay with you.

I am suddenly taken back to an incident at my school when I was about twelve years old. It was in a chemistry lesson, in a science block classroom. I was talking to the boy next to me, when I felt a hard thud and sting on my cheek. I looked up and round to see the chemistry teacher who had slapped me hard across the face. It seemed to come out of nowhere. It was painful for sure, but the shock and humiliation were worse. I was shaking and felt like crying. Ok, I was talking when I shouldn't have been, but so were lots of people. I had simply been singled out as the one to be selected to take the blame or at least punished for the cumulative noise in the room.

As a result, somewhere deep down, an unconscious part of me learned something that day; not just to keep quiet in chemistry lessons, but also that I deserved to be singled out.

TAKE COVER!

That teacher must have chosen me for a reason. At twelve years old, you don't understand that the poor teacher had simply lost control and his selection of you is purely a random consequence – a moment in time. But you never lose that feeling of victimisation, however you attempt to rationalise it in retrospect. Otherwise, why would I remember it after all these years? The memory of physical pain disappears in minutes, but you never forget injustice.

Of course, you'd probably argue it's a good thing that belting kids across the face is now illegal in schools (although some of them do actually deserve it). But I'm even reluctant to visit upon the aforementioned big guy a sense of humiliation and victimisation just because he's the easiest target for blame. As I'm musing over all this (an unusual luxury), the bell rings and I open the door as the class files out. Wandering back to the staff room, I'm thinking what an ironic turn of events. The people in that class probably learned some maths in that cover period with hardly the need for any discipline.

Whereas I learned no chemistry in that lesson over 45 years ago.

GO FOR THE BACK OF THE HEAD

I'm covering an English lesson at Gatesbury School, period 5 and last lesson of the day. There's a rumble that increases in volume as the mob of year 7s (11 to 12-year-olds) approaches down the corridor. As they file in I recognise some of them from previous encounters, and they are not to be messed with. A Teaching Assistant follows them in with an angry look on her face and shouts at a boy who has sat with a group of his fellow cronies at the back:

'Right that's a C3!'

Before leaving me to get on with the class, she explains:

'I asked him to put his water bottle away and he was as rude as could be – so he's now got a C3 and staying behind after school.'

I look over at the boy to see that it's Liam, the pencil stealer, who I gave a C3 to but later retracted a while back. My heart sinks. His mates are goading him:

'Hey Liam that's three C3s you've got now!'

'I don't care – I'm not going to any of them!'

'Get your mum to ring the school.'

'Yeah I will!'

I hold up my hands with arms in the air and introduce myself in my usual fashion, making reference to classroom noise levels:

TAKE COVER!

'Good afternoon.'

'Afternoon Sir!'

'My name is Mr. Webb. Some of you have met me before, some have not…'

At this point I walk amongst them.

'This is the volume at which I speak. I expect the collective volume in this room to be lower than this for the next hour. Is that understood?'

'Yes Sir.'

(Yeah right.)

'Before I tell you what you'll be doing we shall first establish who is here and who is not!'

As I prepare to take the register, there's a scuffle between a boy and a girl who are sitting as a pair in front of my teacher's desk. They are giggling as they fight over a pen. It's mild flirtation but very noisy. Meanwhile Liam and his boys up at the back right hand side of the room are already engaged in various forms of mischief. I look down sternly at the couple in front and raise my eyebrows:

'Thank you!'

They laugh sheepishly but stop.

'Gentlemen at the back – your attention please!'

As I read out the names there are small pockets of disruption here and there, but the class seem to pay attention to the name calling. This is because afterwards, one of them gets to take the completed register down to Student Services where it has to be delivered by law. As we've seen before, this is a much coveted exercise for students, especially younger ones, as it gets them out of the classroom for a few minutes and constitutes a bit of an adventure. After much hand waving and squealing, I tell them that I will count to 3 and the first person with their hand up can be dispatched on this precious duty. Of course, after the count of two a sea of hands are raised and we have to start again. This is actually quite good fun and will probably be the best part of the next hour from my point of view.

SPIKE WEBB

Eventually I choose a winner, Abbie, who jaunts happily out of the room, much to the horror and displeasure of everyone else.

'Sir that's not fair!'
'My hand was up first!'
'No, it was mine!'

I hand out the work that's been left for them, explaining it as I go. I realise that I have deviated from the norm of announcing the instructions from the front beforehand and it's not a good move as it means I can't see everyone. There's a rise in noise levels, some banging of chairs as boys kick under the tables. I'm about to turn and raise my voice when there's a shout from classroom front left:

'Sir – Josh broke my pen, look!'

An angry looking ginger haired boy is holding up a black biro pen which has been split in half and there is black ink all over his hands. The accused is appalled:

'I did NOT!'
'Sir, he did and look at the mess…'

I'm about to try and deal with the situation when a table to my right starts moving. I turn to see a chubby lad with a red face crawl out from underneath:

'What are you doing there? Get back to your seat please!'
'I'm looking for my water bottle Sir!'
'How can you lose something that size? Anyway, it'll have to wait until later…'
'But it's hot and I'm thirsty!'
'I can't help that…'
'Anyway, someone stole it Sir!'
'Just sit down…'

Then there's a loud bang from the other side of the room. I look up and see that a cheeky, gum chewing madam has slammed a heavy text book down on one of the desks. She is armed with many of these and has presumably taken it upon herself to give them out to the rest of the class, having located them at the back of the room. I haven't asked her to do this but figure it'll probably help speed things along. As I turn to re-apply myself to negotiations with the water seeker, there's

TAKE COVER!

another even louder bang, followed by another. Madam is clearly affirming her presence in the room by distributing the books as noisily as possible, a fairly common occurrence when teenagers give out books. Meanwhile, Abbie who took the register down to Student Services has returned and is standing up behind her friend near the classroom door, engaged in the intricate process of plaiting her hair. I move over to her:

'I'm sure your friend here is most gratified by your kind gesture with regard to her hair, but I'm afraid you're going to have to sit down and finish the job later...'

'But Sir, she always let's me do this.'

'Not interested – sit down.'

'You look like Liam Gallagher!'

I move away quickly. I've learnt that firing a command and moving away sometimes emphasises that you are refusing to argue any further and prevents an escalation of conflict, which takes my attention away from other matters. Sometimes it works, sometimes it doesn't. Luckily, I glance round to see that she has sat down. But I know she'll be plaiting that hair again before too long.

I am relieved to see that the chubby guy has made his way back over towards his seat near Liam's mob, minus his water bottle. Just as I return to the front desk to collect my thoughts and attempt to re-establish order, I am confronted by the broken-pen boy from earlier. He shows me his hands which are covered in black ink:

'Sir? Can I go and wash all this ink off?'

'No, you're not supposed to leave the room...'

'But Sir, I'll get it all over the text book and my work sheet.'

I make a snap decision and tell him to go and wash it off and he saunters towards the door, happy at this small victory and a little time out. There's a lot of chat punctuated by yelps as limbs are playfully punched and poked by pens and pencils as I move around the room, attempting to re-iterate what is required of them. The audio levels in the room are made all the more uncomfortable by the fact that none of the boys' voices have broken so the effect is that of incessant high-pitched squealing.

SPIKE WEBB

To make matters worse, I am menaced by the occasional high-pitched screech, a bit like an animal in the middle of a mating ritual or about to go into battle. I'm about to locate the source of this irritant when I'm called over by a girl with a question:

'Sir?'

'Yes?'

'Is there a C for asking a teacher if he's gay?'

'No, not that I know of...'

Someone else chips in:

'I bet there is – there must be!'

'If there is, I'm sure it's not listed on the Consequences chart.'

I can't believe I'm actually actively taking part in this conversation:

'Anyway, back to your task please!'

I turn to see that Abbie the hairdresser is sitting on the desk behind her friend and has resumed her hair plaiting duties. I move briskly over:

'Sit down please and stop...'

'I am sitting down Sir.'

'Sit back down on your chair.'

'I don't want to!'

'Then I'll have to send you out to stand in the corridor.'

Protesting, she slouches back down onto her own seat before enquiring:

'Sir, are you Rod Stewart?'

I'm about to retort with something witty when I see Liam's boys are getting a bit noisy over the other side so I go over to quieten them down. As I approach, my fat water seeker crawls out from under their group of tables and starts looking around frantically at the floor. I'm wondering what can be so important about a plastic bottle of water when he catches my eye. He's quite red-faced and actually looks really worried:

'I've lost my money, Sir!'

'How come?'

'I sold some pens for two quid and now it's gone.'

TAKE COVER!

He delves into his pocket and shows me a handful of coins:

'I had four pounds twenty and now I've only got two twenty so I've lost two quid!'

'Well you'll have to look for it later...'

He's almost pleading now:

'No, it'll be home time and then it'll be too late, I've got to find it now!'

The look of defiance on his face is one of genuine panic, he's sweating, breathless, and I can see he is upset. He continues crawling round on all fours, desperate to find his money. I haven't got the heart to stand in his way as I feel genuinely sorry for him. He reminds me of Piggy in Lord of The Flies.

I remember when I was at school it was always the overweight kid who had the hardest time of it. Not just for being fat. It was as though being fat made everything in life more of a struggle. I was always sorry for the fat guy and I still am now. And anyway, we could both be in the same boat on this battlefield. I've got a train ticket and a few quid in my pocket. If I lost that few quid on this floor, I wouldn't be able to buy a glass of wine to unwind in the pub next to the station on the way home – a relaxing 20 minutes I look forward to every day. The fat guy is probably looking forward to buying crisps or an ice cream for his bus journey home. There's no real difference. I can imagine us both crawling around looking for our cash in the middle of this mayhem:

'Found yours yet?'

'No, any sign of yours?'

And how would we know whose was whose?

'Wait a minute, that's my pound coin!'

The rest of the lesson continues in much the same vein with more dramatic rises in volume checked by sudden shouts for quiet on my part. Some kids are doing the work but finding it hard to blank out the distractions which are relentless in this class. I continue to be plagued by the high-pitched jungle noises and have no idea where they are coming from. At one point, I turn to see the girl who wanted to know if there is a C for asking about gay teachers peering studiously at the Consequences chart on the wall at the entrance of the classroom. I get her to sit back down:

'I told you there's no C for that offence – it probably has consequences though!'

Just before the end of the lesson, a tall girl climbs up onto some shelving units at the back of the room. Before I can stop her, she climbs up still further, reaches behind some reference books and pulls out a plastic bottle of water.

As the bell goes, I stand aside to let this army of uncontrollable, hyperactive year 7s charge out of the room. The last to leave is the fat guy. He's all smiles now:

'I found my money Sir! And my water!'

We leave the classroom together and I watch as he wanders happily off down the corridor. I still feel sorry for him though. It's what I call the 'back of the head' thing. I used to get it with my Dad. He had a lot of problems. Alcohol was one of them. And when I saw him standing with his back to me, or walking off somewhere, contemplating whatever; the world, his world, life, his life, my heart would go out to him. Because from behind, I could see how very vulnerable he was. As of course we all are. I still get it on random occasions these days with people I know and love, and sometimes with strangers who just seem weary and burdened.

And I get the same sad feeling as I watch the fat kid disappear down the corridor. Who knows what he'll eventually make of all this? He's got so much more than a bottle of water and a couple of quid to worry about over the years to come. I'm pleased he got his money back. He's got enough on his plate for now. I hope he enjoys his ice cream.

And I'm looking forward to that glass of wine.

THE WATER BOTTLE — ESSENTIAL KIT FOR EVERY LITTLE SOLDIER

There's a popular game involving plastic bottles with water in. The idea is to toss the bottle in the air, making sure you put a bit of a spin on it, so that hopefully it will have a better chance of landing upright, on its base. The game is called 'flipping', and it's not easy, which is why you have to practice hard to get it right. It requires a certain amount of dedication.

There are also other dimensions to the game. For instance, the aerodynamics change as the level of water contained in the bottle goes down. A quarter-full bottle requires a gentler, more subtle approach to the flip, whereas a three-quarter full bottle needs a more robust delivery. And, of course, there are all the variants in between.

The game can be played pretty well anywhere that has a suitably raised, flat surface. Tables are ideal. So a place where there are lots of tables is the perfect flipping location. The classroom is one such place, and can be quickly converted into an arena in which flipping is played and spectated by many.

Flipping also has great possibilities for expansion. The water in the bottles can be used as a weapon with which to settle any disputes that may arise during the course of the game. In fact, a game of flipping can sometimes become completely abandoned in favour of a water based battle to decide who, at the end of the day, is the overall winner.

When the flipping bottles become empty, they are usually manipulated using a squeezing motion, which creates a cracking sound and serves to celebrate the end of that particular game. It's traditional to do this as opposed to actually applauding.

Flipping is usually officiated over by a marshal, otherwise known as a Cover Support Teacher. However, these marshals don't actually have much power. They are not permitted to restrain the players or even confiscate water bottles if things get a bit out of hand.

Why? Because flipping players have rights. Human rights. And being human means you have certain requirements for survival, the most fundamental of these being water. After all, we all know what happens if you run out of water. Look what happens to people in the desert when they run out of water. If a person is not able to drink water whenever he or she wants, 24/7, he or she could become very ill, or worse. So the marshals must appeal to the flipping players' better sense of judgement in the event of disorder. The only circumstance in which a marshal might be justified in confiscating a water bottle is when it has been emptied and squeezed to such an extent that it has cracked open and cannot be refilled and re-used as a water container.

When officiating at a flipping game, it's often best to adopt a cursory approach, distracting overexcited players with other activities like academic study. Just make sure that they have access to water at all times and that their hydration levels are intact.

As befits their flipping human rights.

ALL QUIET ON ANOTHER FRONT

I'm in a new school. Abbey Cross. I have been told that it used to be a private school. It is a vast, old fashioned rambling building with large front doors that lead into a high ceilinged, regal entrance hall, off which leads a corridor both East or Westwards to a labyrinth of other corridors and classrooms. To the left of the entrance is a reception and enquiries hatch, behind which is an admin office.

A couple of sofas and a small coffee table also feature in the reception area and this morning I notice a nervous looking young student seated with someone who I assume to be his mother waiting to see someone important.

So it seems like a fairly posh place. I am now in class, having selected my cover work for the day from a supply/cover teacher pigeon hole in a particularly large staff room. I have distributed the work and am presiding over thirty year sevens and, for the first time with students of this age, I'm feeling reasonably comfortable. That's because they are impeccably behaved. I can't believe it, and I'm waiting for the catch. Waiting for someone to open fire with a paper plane or flying pencil. Or for someone to start the campaign for mass toilet visits, or the usual breaking of pens and copious ink spillages.

It may be quiet, but I'm still ready to pounce. I'm a little jumpy. But when I do hear a noise it only turns out to be someone unzipping a pencil case or putting a pen down. This unusual, new found classroom euphoria is speckled with paranoia. Suddenly a boy gets up from his seat to talk to a girl at another desk. I'm thinking here we go, that was the calm before the storm. But to my delight he simply asks her a question about the work. And there's not a mobile phone in sight. Just thirty 11 to 12 year olds quietly murmuring to each other about mathematics. Given the varying degrees of mayhem and sometimes completely anarchic behaviour I have often encountered in schools thus far, I'm wondering why these particular youngsters are happy to do the work. Or, at least, if they are not happy with it, they are doing it all the same.

Is it me? Could it be because I'm new here? No. I've been new before and the kids didn't care. They get new cover teachers all the time. Am I giving off a different message? Has my countenance adopted a greater air of confidence and authority? No, I've only been here 20 minutes and they were quiet from the start.

So it's definitely not me. Is it because this is a more affluent area and a posher school? Most people would assume that is the main reason. More money, less despair, less resentment. But why should money make you behave better or more inclined to do something you don't want to for an hour? Surely that makes you more likely to be demanding and intent upon getting your own way. Is it that the real teachers are better at this school? I doubt it. I've seen some real teachers in action in the other schools and some of them are excellent – they just have a hard time of it because they don't have the right disciplinary tools at their disposal.

I'm no expert. There must be loads of studies and socio-scientific reports on all this, but I've never seen any. I didn't get into this with the intention of investigating the varying degrees of effectiveness in modern disciplinary procedures at secondary schools. I came here to get money to pay some bills and buy Guinness. So I don't pretend to know the answers. But there's one thing I do notice as these well-behaved youngsters file out at the end of the lesson.

There's not a consequences chart in sight.

CALLING FOR REINFORCEMENTS

It's period 4, the one before lunch, so everyone's a bit tired. I'm in a science lab at Leaton Down school and a bunch of year 10s are filing in and taking their places on stools around three large, high work benches. I am to distribute some work sheets on which are a series of interrelated shapes and a colour-coded table along the bottom. I haven't had time to study the intricacies of these tasks but, suffice to say, the students are required to use coloured felt pens to fill in the shapes, thus revealing a picture that is hitherto cleverly concealed. It seems to me to be a ridiculously easy task to put upon a fifteen-year-old person, unless that person is seriously backward or disabled. These students seem to be perfectly able, some of them may be quite bright. I can't really say as I've never taken this class before as it's my newest school, but although they are quite lively, they seem quite happy to get down to the colouring in.

Before the lesson, the science teacher whose classroom it is had given me the low down on what to do if there are any problems. I simply need to knock on the door at the back of the room behind which she will be, working at her computer in a small office and storeroom. This has made me a little wary, because not only does it imply that things could get a bit hairy, it also means that she will be witness to my inability to contain a situation on my own. Call it misplaced pride if you like, but I hate the idea of appearing incapable of coping, perhaps because part of me knows that I'm a bit of an imposter, having drifted into this line of work out of need as opposed to any initial vocational calling.

I'm pacing around the room, musing over this. I don't like to overcrowd the students, so occasionally, I look at some of the stuff on the walls at the back of the room, especially if things are fairly calm. So I'm staring at a poster depicting the anticipated outcomes of various chemicals when mixed together, sometimes rightly, sometimes wrongly. I remember not being very good at chemistry at school, probably because I just wasn't interested. But I certainly don't remember being given something to colour in instead. As a teenager, I might have seen that as a bit of an insult. My thoughts are digressing in the relative quiet of the classroom, and I'm relieved that we're off to a good start and it looks as though I'm not going to have to knock on that lady science teacher's door.

Then it happens. I hear the crash of wood on metal. I jump in alarm and look round to see two students gripped in a fight near my teacher's desk at the front. A real fight. Not the playful silly stuff you sometimes get, but serious conflict. They are kicking, punching, grappling. As I rush over one gets the other in a headlock, they surge backwards and crash into a metal cabinet, knocking test tubes, bottles of liquid and exercise books to the floor. Beetroot with rage, the guy in the headlock knees his opponent in the balls which sparks even more flying fists and boots as they crash into more cabinets and work benches. Other students are shouting for them to stop, because it's actually quite frightening. These guys are virtually grown men, and they are strong, able and clearly willing to do each other considerable damage.

I am unable to pull them apart as I am not allowed to touch them. So I rush to the door at the back of the room, open it and enter, but the cupboard is bare. The science teacher has simply disappeared. As I turn back into the classroom, I see that order has been partially restored. The fight has been stopped by two other students, who are holding the fighters apart, and they seem to be calming down. Inwardly shocked and slightly

TAKE COVER!

shaken, I address the class in the manner of one who is fully composed and clearly used to dealing with this kind of thing:

'Ok, we have a choice here. I can call someone to come and investigate this incident and find out who started it, or would you prefer me to pretend it never happened?'

They nod in assent at the latter.

'Ok, I'll pretend it never happened on condition that the rest of this lesson continues without even the slightest incident, understood?'

Much relieved, they take their seats and recommence their colouring-in in earnest. I glance to see that the two involved in the fight are both still red-faced with what I assume to be a combination of anger and embarrassment. They are sitting apart, something which has been stealthily re-organised by the peacemakers who eventually held them apart. I return to the front of the class, relieved on the one hand that the rest of the lesson will be without any messing about to deal with, but also a little nervous of the possibility the two enemies may well decide to clash again. As I'm taking the opportunity to jot some of this down on a piece of paper on my front teacher's desk, one of the perpetrators gets up and slowly makes for the door.

'Excuse me, where are you going?'

I am completely ignored as he leaves the room. I follow him out to see him calmly descending the spiral staircase that leads down to the atrium and out of the science block. I can't go after him because that would mean leaving the class unattended, so I have no choice but to let him go.

After about ten minutes a member of the school's student support staff enters the class and pulls me aside.

'Just to let you know I've got Jordan – I found him wandering around the courtyard. Don't worry, he's one of mine. I'll take care of him.'

He goes on to explain that Jordan is slightly autistic and prone to erratic behavior. So the likelihood is that Jordan struck out at his victim for no apparent reason, which makes me feel even more sorry for the other lad, who's still a bit red in the face. Soon the bell goes and I open the science lab door as they all file out, slightly subdued, which is a first during my time as a cover support teacher.

On the bus on the way home, again I'm wondering about the wisdom of putting a complete stranger in charge of a class of 15-year-olds, one of whom suffers from autism and is likely to attack someone else at any random moment. I don't know them, and I haven't been briefed on the possibility of real violence occurring. That's hardly surprising, because if you tell someone they are likely to find themselves having to stop a real fight and prevent serious damage, chances are they'd chicken out. And as for the woman teacher who was supposed to be on hand in case of trouble?

Call me old-fashioned, but I remember a time when individuals who are unfortunate enough to suffer from these conditions used to attend places where one-to-one supervision and specialist care was administered, not bunged amongst a load of other kids, any of whom could be the unsuspecting victim of a random attack at any time. Some people might say that such a person's human rights dictate that he/she has a right to be integrated with normal kids at school. If that's the case, then surely teachers, cover teachers, supply staff and the students themselves should be fully trained in martial arts skills as a matter of course, as would befit their own human rights to defend themselves. And then there's the other problem, people in authority in schools are not allowed to physically touch a student, whatever he or she is doing. So you would end up with a whole load of teenagers fully trained in unarmed combat being watched by teachers and support staff who can only watch as they sort it all out themselves.

So what's the answer? I'm not qualified to say. After all I'm just a drummer. But I could tentatively offer a suggestion. Perhaps it should be acknowledged that kids who are likely to behave like loose cannons should be properly looked after, not set among unsuspecting people who could fall victim to physical assault at any time. Stop using the human rights slogan as a shield behind which to impose ridiculous measures on important institutions so that you can save money by closing down all the institutions which were originally

TAKE COVER!

established to help people with uncontrollable difficulties in the first place. But at the end of the day, it does all boil down to economics.

Which is why I'll be back in school tomorrow.

HIDDEN WEAPON

Monday morning, Ashfields school, on the really rough estate. I'm at my usual position, at the front of class, having taken a turn around the room to do the usual round of policing work. Pens leaking, phones appearing then being hidden, girls giggling about what happened on Friday night. This lot of year nines are quite boisterous and have no intention of applying themselves to the geographical study sheets I have distributed.

For some reason, it has been requested that the door to the classroom be left open for the beginning of the lesson. However, it serves to remind me of just how quiet it is in the other classrooms on this floor. As ever, this makes me feel acutely inadequate in comparison. Ok, so everyone knows a cover support teacher's job is virtually impossible due to the nature of the lesson, but I still want to be seen to be in control. And the noise is getting louder. There's one lad who's getting particularly animated about his exploits at the weekend. I saunter over.

'Come on, let's get some of these questions answered on the sheet.'

'What questions Sir?'

'The ones on the sheets in front of you...'

'We don't know anything about these – we've never studied them!'

'You mean they're for a different class?'

He shrugs. Then the girl behind pipes up.

'I've seen them before Sir!'

TAKE COVER!

'So how come he hasn't?'

'I used to be in a different class for geography...'

Then there's a commotion at the back of the room. An argument has ensued as the result of a game of cards. I walk over and insist the cards are put away, which causes much remonstration and not a little mirth.

I decide to return to the front of the room and lay it on the line as best I can by raising my voice in a general appeal to young budding adults to consider the finer points of good behavior, especially in classrooms. But before I get the chance to speak, in strolls a man who I will refer to as the Clint Eastwood of secondary schools. Don't get me wrong, he's not wearing a cowboy hat or a poncho and he's not smoking a cheroot. Nothing could be further from the truth. He is an ordinary, casually suited individual. His countenance is that of a relaxed and calm visitor to this classroom.

However, the effect he has on the entire class is remarkable. There is suddenly complete silence as every student begins to study the geography sheets in front of them. You could hear a pin drop. All these teenagers are clearly terrified of this man as he sits down at an empty desk and looks around the room. Looking at him, I can't fathom why. He's not a big bloke, and he hasn't said a word.

This man has clearly heard the rising din from the corridor and decided to help me out by quietening things down to complete silence for a while. The effect his presence has on this class is simply unbelievable. I'm wondering what it is they are all so in awe of. The thing is, he didn't even need to say anything. I'm thinking has he actually got a gun?

After a while, Clint gets up and leaves. And once he's safely out of earshot, the noise naturally begins again, because little old me definitely does not have that kind of clout. Under normal teaching circumstances, that guy clearly takes no prisoners. It must take a certain type of person to have that kind of control. Or some seriously good training. A far cry from the kind of mayhem that holds sway in cover lessons. Then I have an idea. Maybe tomorrow I'll bring a lifelike pistol into the next cover lesson and place it on the teacher's desk in front of me, laughing menacingly.

But when it comes to consequences, that would be way off the richter scale.

RUBBER BULLETS

Red-faced and beetroot with anger, the woman bellows at the top of her screechy voice into the fray. She's like a machine gun trained on the crowd. Every now and then, she bellows at them. But she's firing blanks; no-one seems to be taking any notice.

The year 9 students waiting outside the Maths classroom that I'm about to enter are largely ignoring her, as though it's a familiar backdrop to their pushing, jostling, gossiping, Facebooking, snapchatting, whatsapping and whatever else occupies them as they wait to be instructed in GCSE Mathematics. Still she shouts, like a wild woman on a mission. On seeing me approach, the students get excited as they know it's going to be a cover lesson.

'Ah great – are you taking us Sir?'
'Yes It would seem so.'
'Can we listen to music?'
'You look like Simon Cowell.'
Simon *Cowell*?
The wild woman interjects loudly:
'Be quiet! Wait until Sir's ready then file in quietly in a line!'

* * *

I enter the classroom and look at the work sheets that have been left on the teacher's desk. As usual, I struggle to make head or tail of what they are supposed to be doing. I'm also aware that exercise books and text books need to be given out. But first I must take the register. I also know, as they do, that this is widely regarded as a non-lesson, a fiasco during which I go through the motions of giving out work, that work being largely ignored, negotiating requests to visit the toilet, fill water bottles, listen to music etc. I'll walk up and down, trying to encourage them, stopping multiple play-fights, picking up paper airplanes, stopping people moving seats and breaking up mobile phone groove music parties.

I want to establish some kind of satisfactory relationship with them, whereby we do a kind of deal. They make some effort to do some work in return for some privileges. The problem is, I can't because the wild woman is in here, shouting at them sporadically, which is also largely ignored. But if I try and appeal to their better natures, it will contravene the stance she has already taken and is known for taking every day, all day long, wherever she happens to be sent by the Teacher's Assistants department. I've been in lessons with her before on a number of occasions. She is even more furious with Year 7 and 8s, as they are noisy and uncontrollable in a more frantic and unpredictable way.

What is really disturbing is that this wildly angry, permanently furious woman is potentially the most frightening individual in the whole building, yet no-one takes any notice of her. They might moan a bit if she gives a C3, which is quite often, but that's about the only reaction her manic bellowing ever achieves. She dishes out C1s like parking tickets, but no-one seems to care. So what kind of message is the school giving out to students? That a Consequences chart, a possible chinwag with the parents and a mad woman shouting at them, is about as bad as it gets?

As I'm wondering what strategy to deploy, the shouting woman gets up to leave:

'I have an appointment in another class, Sir – if you have any trouble, be sure to call Student Services.'

I've been told that before and so remain confused; there is no phone in the classroom and even if there was I don't have the extension number for Student Services. I would be

TAKE COVER!

reluctant to call anyway as it would be admitting defeat (I later learn that calls to that department are made by a variety of teachers and cover support people on a regular basis so there's actually no shame in it).

The shouting woman has left me with a problem though. I either carry on with the now established stern approach, or I go back to my usual style (if you can call it that) which is to try and win them over by being reasonable. Have some conversations, some fun even. But if you want to achieve proper discipline, maybe the stern approach is the only real option at the end of the day, even though the legal restrictions that apply with regard to discipline make that approach a bit like trying to control a rabid dog on Blue Peter.

After taking the register and sending the lucky winner of my 'hands up first' game to take it to Student Services, the class get lively with cheeky questions:

'Sir? Are you Rod Stewart?'

Clearly that begs another question from me:

'Why would I be here trying to control you lot if I was wearing it as well as him?'

Then I think of a better response:

'Yes actually, I am. I felt it was time for a career move so I decided to stop singing and shout at teenagers instead. You know, give something back and all that.'

Fast forward to later that afternoon and I'm walking past the Gatesbury School playing fields with a young PE teacher on our way to the gym (where I am required for legal reasons) and a bunch of year nines are playing football. Suddenly there's applause and cheering from some of the lads and one of them shouts out:

'Alright Rod?'

Then he runs up to me and insists on hi-fiving before running back to his game. I smile apologetically to the gym teacher.

'Sorry about that, some of them like to nick name me Rod. I don't know why – my hair I suppose.'

'It's because they like you – you obviously make them feel comfortable.'

SPIKE WEBB

'Really? I was worried it might be a problem.'

'Quite the opposite. It's really encouraging to see!'

'Perhaps Rod Stewart makes people feel comfortable too?'

We laugh and continue to the gym. But as I'm supervising the gym teacher supervising twenty or so teenage girls, I'm feeling a bit encouraged. Chuffed even. Because up until now I'd been thinking that being pally with students might seem like a sign of weakness. I've hi-fived several students in the corridors as the celebrated 'Rod' before, nervous of being seen by other teachers who might consider it a sign of someone who's not taking their position as a cover support teacher seriously. So, to be told it's not a bad thing is a bit of a relief.

It also takes me back to my own school days. As a teenage school kid, I'd always get other kids from different classes and even different years calling out my recently acquired nick name 'Spike!' in the corridors between lessons. The only difference now is it's 'Rod'.

And it's nice to feel popular among relative strangers again. Even if it is principally because of one's apparent similarity in appearance to someone else, it might mean they actually like me.

I'm musing over all this again as I'm sitting in a big Wetherspoon pub early that evening, waiting to wander down and start my evening cleaning job at six o'clock. Suddenly I hear a comment from behind where I'm sitting:

'You look like Rod Stewart!'

I look round to see an attractive young woman walking up the stairs towards the loos. Then laughing, she adds:

'Especially from behind!'

I laugh out loud:

'A lot of people say that!'

I saunter down to the offices where I clean in an unusually upbeat mood. It's ok to be liked by students, maybe the soft approach works better for some. And now I have a nick name at school again. Instead of 'Sir' I'm 'Rod'.

Perhaps it should be 'Sir Rod'.

BOGGED DOWN

I'm pushing the rotating doors of the office building where I do my cleaning job for two hours every evening from 6 until 8pm. It seems like ages ago since I left the school gates at 3.20 earlier this afternoon. And, as always, the day seems a bit of a blur. I'd forgotten how packed full school days are. Five hours of lessons, trials, tribulations, battles fought, lessons learned or not as the case may be, conflicts, triumphs, tantrums, all the usual stuff. And today has been a full day as I've been covering all periods without any free periods. So I am especially relieved to climb the stairs to the first floor office toilets, push open the hefty fire door to the familiar humming sound of the main frame computer server in the computer room just off the corridor. I make my way to the end of a corridor, past the men's toilets to the ladies, in which is located the walk-in cleaning store closet. I like the comforting routine of entering this pantry-type room which contains all the cleaning stuff and putting on a pair of cheap, surgical rubber gloves from the multi-pack provided.

Most people would sigh in anticipation of two hours rigorous cleaning, and sometimes I do, but today I'm sighing with relief because it's a chance for me to hide again. Yes, I can hide in these toilets, as though I have escaped from school and, in a small way, I am escaping from being skint. As I splash the large vanity mirror above the first set of wash basins in the ladies, I muse about people at school, my cover friends, the other teachers, the students, the kids. Liam, Taylor, Jack the loose cannon, Abbie the hair platter.

Then, when I finish the mirrors, taps and basins and get into the toilets themselves, I can really start to let the tension out. I come across a stubborn piece of yellowy-brown human excrement on the inside rim of a toilet bowl. I curse, of course, because on the surface of things it is horrible. But actually, I like it because it's a different kind of challenge. A battle even. And it's one I know I can win.

So I scrub hard. Some of it dislodges, but not all, so I must scrub harder. This piece of faeces is particularly stubborn. It's quite dry and very hard in texture and I'm thinking it may have been there for a while. I don't remember it from last night though. Anyway it's got to go. I manage to remove some of the yellow which is a partial victory, but the brown just won't budge.

I start to get quite cross, but it's a good kind of cross, not the kind of cross I can get in the classroom, where I'm stressed, confused and not sure if I will prevail. In this environment, I know I will prevail. And if a piece of shit gets particularly disobedient, I boost my determination by imagining it represents something I detest and need to eradicate: self-doubt, guilt, proper joblessness, failure.

Then, if it still persists, I imagine it's an illness someone has, someone I know. So now this persistent, human botty stain has become cancer. A piece of cancer. It's really had it now, it's got to go. So I refresh my paper cloth with cleaning fluid and scrub harder than ever. Sweat is pouring down my cheeks as I deliver one final push to win the ultimate battle.

Sure enough, eventually it gives in and is gone. Every vile thing it stood for: frustration, stress, insecurity, worry, cancer, all eradicated for a brief moment in time, before the next piece of crap comes along.

If only you could get rid of life's bigger problems as easily as that.

As I rush eagerly into the next cubicle, I am aware, for an instant, of the possibility that I may be going a little insane. But by the time I get out of the toilets on the first and ground

TAKE COVER!

floors and out onto the floor cleaning tasks in reception and then onto vacuuming and mopping the canteen floor, the end part of the job, I've forgotten about school, and most of my worries. I've cleaned it all away, until tomorrow that is, when the whole process starts again.

But one thing's for sure, when you've got worries you can't do much about, there's nothing like cleaning up someone else's shit to make you feel better.

TAKING COMMAND

St Christopher Academy, afternoon lesson before home time. I've arrived at the classroom a little early after lunch to get prepared before the students gather outside the door. This afternoon's subject is English Literature, specifically Romeo and Juliette by William Shakespeare. The play is available for study reference in the form of text book paperbacks, thirty of which are stacked in a cabinet next to the classroom door. I have my lesson instructions as to which act and scene for the class to refer to when answering the questions listed on the cover work sheet, which I shall arrange to have distributed when the register has been taken. Somewhat unusually, everything has been pre-arranged rather well and it's now crystal clear what this class is required to do for the next fifty minutes.

So what could possibly go wrong?

Soon the sound of bustling feet and general merriment approaches and, although everything is all ready to go, I brace myself, for the rapid accumulation of fifteen-year-olds outside a door has a foreboding effect. I open the door and, wearing my 'stern to start with but nice bloke really' face, invite the good people to enter. There is a mass-saunter into the room as I return to my position at the teacher's desk. The students busy themselves in selecting the best possible places to sit for an afternoon's fun and entertainment as they have, by now, quickly recognised this as a cover lesson and thus a free period. Of course, I've seen it all before countless times, and there's

TAKE COVER!

nothing different about this. I wonder if being better prepared with the work at hand actually makes any difference at all when it comes to fifteen-year-olds. Younger years do appreciate a little preparation and can sometimes respond to what you're asking of them (in small pockets, amid surrounding mayhem) but pubescent men and women just aren't interested.

However, I am further dismayed when one particular individual asserts himself as one who will not be controlled my another under any circumstances. Well, certainly not these. Before sitting down, he strides up to me with a wide grin on his face.

'Alright Sir? Had a good day?'

'Yes thank you, please take your seat with the others.'

With that, I walk to the centre front to address the class, who are still bustling about to get seated. To my surprise and dismay, the lad who approached me has sat himself down in the chair at the teacher's desk, legs stretched out in the manner of one who might be reposing at home after a long, hard day.

I turn to him:

'Come on, you can't sit there.'

'Why not?'

'Because that's the teacher's chair. Go and sit with the others.'

Then a voice from a boy at the back:

'Nathan, come and sit with us!'

Luckily, Nathan seems up for that and saunters over to the back of the room. However, instead of sitting amongst his friends, he places his chair a little forward, so that he is able to turn and communicate with them but has his full focus on me. It's a kind of intimidation, but always there is this wide grin on his face. As I introduce myself in the usual fashion (mentioning noise volumes etc) and take the register, Nathan settles down and adopts the pose of one who is about to enjoy being entertained by an amateur comedian. Occasionally, he shouts out a witty remark which is usually quite funny. Not obscene or offensive, just amusing and slightly provocative – as people often do when they are in the audience at a comedy club.

SPIKE WEBB

What makes this even harder from my point of view is that the remarks, my responses, and indeed the whole situation is quite funny. But I need to retain composure, so I try and establish a reasonable rapport with Nathan and the class without actually laughing.

Thankfully, after a while Nathan gets restless and joins his comrades at the back of the class to engage in other forms of tomfoolery too varied to mention here. Although the class have the list of questions pertaining to Romeo and Juliette on their cover work sheets, I decide to put a stamp on my position of authority by reading them out clearly and with decisive volume before also writing them on the board.

Of course, very few people are in the slightest bit interested. However, I manage to get certain responses from the quieter, less bumptious types by approaching them and asking my own questions about the play:

'I don't know much about Romeo and Juliette – is it quite tragic?'

'Yes, Sir! They both get killed!'

'Wow, what bit are you on then?'

'The balcony scene, Sir.'

'Is that the famous part that everyone knows? Romeo, Romeo, Wherefore art though…?'

'That's right, Sir!'

These brief interludes are soon brought to a halt by my having to attend a rise in over-zealous, boisterous behaviour from other parts of the room, most frequently Nathan and his boys.

As ever, my glances at the clock on the wall become more and more frequent as the lesson progresses. I notice with dismay that boredom levels have risen to such a degree that the good old paper airplanes start to appear and it's time for me to intercept the odd one in mid-flight. One such example has been expertly crafted by Nathan who, of course, is the best paper plane designer of all. Well, at fifteen years old, with four years' academy practice anyone should have mastered that particular art by now.

I approach with a resigned but determined gait:

TAKE COVER!

'Come on Nathan, it might be impressive but let's keep it out of the air for now...'

'I'm not going to launch it, Sir. I'm going to keep it.'

I know what will happen as soon as my back is turned, so I take decisive action and swiftly remove it from his hand before putting it on the teacher's desk:

'You can have it back at the end of the lesson.'

Nathan seems perfectly happy with this, partly because during the course of the afternoon we seem to have established a reasonable rapport.

But then Nathan does something extraordinary.

He stands up, walks to the front of the class and removes one of about fifty post it notes from a noticeboard next to the whiteboard. He suddenly asserts himself as someone in complete authority and, reading from the piece of paper, with deep voiced confidence, he addresses the entire class:

'How does Romeo express his love for Juliet?'

The class eagerly shout out the answer.

He drops the post-it note and pulls off another:

'What city is Romeo and Juliet set in?'

The class answer in unison:

'VERONA!'

Another post-it:

'Where does the sword fight take place?'

'MANTUA!'

I stare at Nathan in amused disbelief as he continues to tear the post-its from the noticeboard and shout out questions, while the whole class excitedly shout out the answers. Although my authority has been completely usurped, what's happening is more constructive than I could possibly have imagined. This young, cocky individual has successfully taken control of a rowdy classroom with expert, consummate ease. The only downside is that he is simply dropping the post-it notes onto the floor when he's read out the questions.

Well, you can't have everything.

Then, suddenly the classroom door opens abruptly and in march two members of SLT. I should explain here that SLT are School Leadership Teams whose special responsibilities vary but incorporate a certain amount of attention to school discipline. These are the people often called upon to come and restore order if things get out of hand, particularly if someone needs removing from the class. In this instance, however, they are simply passing and checking that all is well. Although seemingly unperturbed, Nathan nevertheless sits back down immediately.

'Is everything ok, Sir?'

I answer a little sheepishly:

'Yes, thank you.'

The situation thus diffused, it's now time to pack up as it's two minutes to the bell and home time. As usual, I open the door for the class as the bell rings and they file/rush out, some playfighting on the way. As Nathan walks past, we nod to each other, smiling:

'Thank you, Sir!'

'Until next time, Nathan!'

I decide to pick up some pieces of screwed-up paper, the odd airplane and discarded pens to make the room a bit more presentable the next day before making my way to reception to sign out for the day.

On the bus I'm reflecting over what happened at the end of that lesson. In retrospect, it was quite extraordinary. It was as if Nathan had simply had enough of the general futility of the lesson, or even cover periods in general, and decided to show his exasperation by taking over:

'Oh, for fxxx's sake, we've learnt all this before, it's not rocket science. Look I'll show you – listen up everyone – let's show Sir here what a waste of time this all is!'

Whatever his reasons for taking over like that, the fact remains he was really good at it. He had taken complete control of the class without the slightest effort – it seemed totally natural to him. At fifteen he'll have his GCSEs next year. Of course, I have no idea what he's good at or how well or otherwise he's expected to do. Given his performance towards the end of the lesson, he might make a good teacher – but that's probably the last thing he wants to do.

TAKE COVER!

Of course, I have no idea how he behaves with proper teachers. For all I know, he might have a terrible reputation for being out of control, or alternatively he might be a lively but keen student who simply sees cover lessons as futile and a pointless waste of everyone's time. Anyway, I'm not often sent to this school so I'll probably never see him again. One thing's for sure though, this young man has taught me something. As well as dealing with all the predictable classroom tricks, antics and acts of defiance that are a well-established part of cover lessons, there's something else a cover teacher should always remember to do...

...expect the unexpected.

PREPARING TO ADVANCE

I'm in a maths revision class for five year 11 students at Gatesbury. They are in the process of preparing for their GCSE in mathematics, which will take place in two weeks. After that, depending on their results, and of course the results of all their other GCSE subjects, they will decide upon their immediate future. And ultimately, begin their chosen journey into what lies beyond.

But there is a problem. This small group of sixteen-year-old boys/men are really bad at maths, and probably other subjects too. That's why there are only five of them. They need special attention, which they are getting from a Teaching Assistant who is also in the room, and I can tell she's a good teacher. I will later learn that their classroom behavior in earlier years has been so appalling that it is astonishing that they've managed to make it this far. But that's all behind them now, they've come through all that. But the damage has been done. It is also highly likely that their relative solitude is to do with them not hindering the chances of other students.

They seem like a nice bunch. They are cheeky and disinclined to do any studying, but they've grown out of the disruptive, anti-authority phase and genuinely understand that the teachers have their best interests at heart. It's just too late, that's all. The Teaching Assistant is helping them with their revision work and she seems to know them fairly well and most

TAKE COVER!

importantly, they like her. She has the ability to strike the right balance between enjoying a joke, joining in with their quirkiness on the brink of adulthood while at the same time encouraging them to do some work, something they would have absolutely no intention of doing if I was alone in the room with them. And why should they? I'm not a maths teacher so I can't help them or encourage them. This assistant clearly is and can back up her occasional revision prompting by being able to give practical help.

There is a little swearing every now and then, but it's real swearing, not the rebellious, showoffy type stuff that comes from younger students. There would be no point in threatening a C3 for bad language as it would also threaten the equilibrium that has been achieved in this revision class. The Teaching Assistant has got it right. So right, in fact, that there is clearly no need for me to be here at all, which is a bit embarrassing. I feel a bit of a fraud as I pace around the room in an attempt to appear important. There is no point in my pulling them up on swearing, the occasional joke or chatting with Miss about the weekend because that would be undermining everything she has already achieved in other sessions. So I am, without doubt, surplus to all requirements except, of course, the legal one.

I listen as the silence is regularly broken with chat that moves from cars and football, back to maths, on to lager strengths and sexual innuendo, back to maths, then on to Donald Trump, then the European Cup, the local job situation and again back to maths. Then the noisiest boy called Josh makes an announcement:

'There's a lot of money in people trafficking.'

The Teaching Assistant is horrified:

'Don't be stupid, Josh! What good is a load of money if you're in prison?'

'I'll tunnel my way out!'

Of course Josh isn't serious. He's simply fleshing out his frustrations on finding himself on the brink of a bleak reality that looms on his own horizon.

There is silence again as they get back to their maths. After a minute or so Josh breaks it again:

SPIKE WEBB

'There's seriously big money in that.'

'That's enough Josh!'

Silence again until:

'Miss? How old do you have to be to go down the job centre?'

'You could go straight after your exams if you want to.'

'What do I need to take with me? Identification and stuff?'

I decide to interject:

'You might find a GCSE in maths quite useful...'

Although the Teaching Assistant heartily agrees, I immediately regret the comment because I realise it's unfair. It's a cheap shot. These people have virtually no hope of getting decent grades in maths and my remark is pure flippancy, so I try and lighten it up:

'Although apparently you need maths GCSE to work at MacDonald's these days.'

They all laugh and I am redeemed.

It turns out that Josh actually wants to join the army. But he states emphatically that unlike all the other boys who say they want to join the army, he really means it. It's the first time I've heard him speak seriously about anything and I can tell by his voice he is concerned about his future.

The bell goes and I open the door for Miss and the boys/men to leave. Miss smiles on her way out:

'Thank you, Sir.'

'It is I who should be thanking you!'

They file out, relieved to have the lesson over with. I watch as Josh heads off down the corridor to his next lesson, one more step towards whatever future he has. The army, MacDonald's, who knows? But I genuinely hope it works out for him. Whatever circumstances have led to his underdevelopment academically and however much he may or may not be to blame, he still deserves a chance. I can see that in the midst of it all he's got a lot to give.

It just has nothing to do with maths.

TAKE COVER!

* * *

As I wander out of the school gates, nodding and smiling politely to the head teacher who seems to appear at the end of most school days to greet people as they exit, students and teachers alike, shaking hands with the odd parent or visitor as if the whole affair has been a kind of celebratory open day, I'm wondering about teenagers like Josh who will most likely leave school behind them with no qualifications whatsoever. Many apply to do college courses which they take marginally more seriously than school, and perhaps find a path towards a future trade, skill or maybe something sporting or musical.

    Then on the bus, I'm musing over what I did when I first left school. I was lucky enough to have a grammar school education at a time when college wasn't an immediate option. The focus was on getting into university, and I managed to get a place at Sheffield University.

    But I didn't go…

FLASHBACK: GAINFUL EMPLOYMENT

Monday morning. About 8am and a bit fresh outdoors. Well, it was kind of outdoors in a half-covered annexe to a factory unit on an industrial estate just outside my hometown of Bushey. It was the beginning of my second week as a metal jig stripper. This meant in the first instance putting painted metal rods into acid baths to soak. The idea was that the dangerously powerful acid would weaken the paint so that it could be easily hosed off. So after some time, wearing my special industrial rubber gloves, I would remove the rods from the baths and throw them on the concrete floor. Then (and this is the bit I liked) I would stand some six feet away and blast them with a high powered industrial hose until all the paint was washed away, leaving just the bare metal jigs.

I was working with another guy roughly my age of 18 years. He did the same thing. There were hundreds of these jigs so plenty to go round. This occupied us from 8 until 5 with a 4pm finish on Friday, 2 tea breaks of 15 minutes and half an hour for lunch. We had no problem observing these strict timing schedules as they were vigorously signified by a loud and vaguely offensive hooting noise that resounded around the building. Our arrival and departure times were regulated with similar efficiency by an arrangement that involved inserting your personal card into the clocking machine on entering and leaving the building.

TAKE COVER!

On the Friday morning my companion asked me if I had any qualifications. When I told him I had recently acquired some GCE's at A and O level he suggested that I use them to get away from the smell of the acid.

So I left. It was my first job on leaving school. I had been offered a place at Sheffield University to study English Literature but had decided to take a year off to become a pop star.

That afternoon I went back to my folks' house where my mates and I hung around in the street smoking fags. It was 1977, a hot summer and, at 18 years old, a fairly carefree one. And although I had done fairly well at Watford Boys Grammar School, I considered myself to be first and foremost a drummer. I was in a band and we rehearsed every week at my friend's house and did a few gigs locally. But of course, the intention was to 'make it' somehow.

In the meantime I was offered another job at an office in Watford working for a company that sold garden furniture and fancy domestic appliances via their brochure and telephone sales. It was through a friend of mine from the same school and same gang of street smokers. It had been decided that my role at the office would be unspecified to begin with, adopting an initially modular approach until I had discovered my particular area of expertise, at which time my function would become more clearly defined. I think I had a short meeting with an important person who gave me a vague idea of what the company did but I seem to remember finding it a little difficult to grasp any detail. I was allocated a tiny desk which was positioned adjacent to two other proper desks that faced each other, so I was temporarily bolted on to the more established proceedings of everyday office life.

I was given some fairly minor administrative tasks to do while I used my vantage point to watch what my colleagues were doing and listen to their phone calls. They seemed to be mainly deployed to deal with enquiries with regard to the company's merchandise and money saving offerings, which of course became all the more elaborate the longer the potential customer stayed on the phone. Unfortunately, my admin work was a little lacklustre and it was soon decided that I should be shown another side to the company's everyday functionality.

I was shown into another office where I was introduced to a rather cross looking Asian man. Also in the room was a young girl putting various pieces of A4 paper with different things typed on them in different positions around the room.

The Asian man explained that this is where we 'split' the orders. This was new to me, as I didn't actually know what an order was, let alone how to split one. He showed me a batch of A4 sheets of paper which had tables showing product names, part numbers and quantities with pricing and discount details. These sheets had a strange kind of crinkly blue paper between them. He explained that carbon paper was used to create copies of the orders in triplicate: one for the customer, one for the order department and one for company records. He showed me how to gently separate the order and carbon copies from the carbon paper, thus freeing them up for reallocation.

Then it was my turn.

"Here, you have a go."

I nervously held a triplicate order and prepared to disengage the copies, starting at the top. Unfortunately I was a little over zealous in my approach and ended up tearing the papers straight down the middle, carbon and all.

So I had literally 'split' the order, from top to bottom.

"Oh, er, sorry."

My instructor's expression was a combination of horror and disbelief. He didn't say much, he simply took my ripped order and left the room. The young girl was smirking. She had clearly mastered the whole thing ages ago and knew the ins and outs of order splitting like the back of her hand.

The rest of my first week continued in much the same vein and on the Friday I was summoned to the finance director's office. He looked downcast, almost sad.

"I hate this part of my job, but unfortunately I have to do it."

"Oh!"

TAKE COVER!

"I'm afraid things haven't gone quite as we'd hoped and we don't think that, in the long run, office work is for you. I'm afraid we're going to have to go our separate ways."

I was overjoyed.

"We will, of course, pay you for this past week without tax up until the end of today."

"Ok, thanks, great."

"Sorry and good luck."

My week's pay without tax was twenty-five pounds.

So early that evening I was back in the street smoking with my mates and the good news was I had some money to go to the pub with, which was unusual for me.

And, of course, I was going to be a pop star drummer.

FLASHBACK: BASHING BOXES — THREE MONTHS' HARD LABOUR

My next foray into the world of gainful employment came in November that year when I accepted a temporary position as a stockroom porter at Watford's British Home Stores. My job was to help out behind the scenes over the Christmas period. After a few days mucking in with some other lads (some of whom I still know to this day) clearing up mess from the shop floor, moving stock around in the stockroom, taking rubbish out to the yard etc, I was selected to occupy another position. Something more specific.

I was to be a baler.

This meant that I was more or less permanently installed in the baling room which is where empty boxes of all shapes and sizes would be deposited throughout the day. My job was to jump up and down on them, crushing them down as far as possible. Then I would throw them into a huge metal machine through a kind of side hatch which I closed up when the machine was full. Then I pressed a red button and a loud engine sound would fire up as a vast internal plunger would

TAKE COVER!

descend within and crush all the cardboard down into something the size of a bale of hay.

Once the machine had finished crushing, I would open the lower side doors and begin the laborious task of feeding plastic tape through holes from one side to the other and tying up the bale of cardboard. This done, I placed it onto a British Home Stores stacking pallet. When there were about three bales on the pallet, it was time to take them via the internal lift to the outside yard, where they would be collected. This could take a while as the lifts got quite congested.

When I got back to my baling room there would inevitably be dozens more boxes to crush and the more frantically I jumped on them, the quicker the boxes came flying into the room. I quickly realised that if, once I'd crushed them, I ripped the boxes up into smaller, flatter pieces, I could get more into the machine, meaning fewer bales and trips to the yard.

You see, my problem was I wanted to go home on time, especially on a Friday if I had a gig to play in the evening. But this particular job meant that things would stack up right at the end of the day. Overtime was kind of compulsory as Mr Cook (Cookie) insisted that the place be clear of cardboard before the machine was switched off. So if there was a moment when I was box free, I would leave my position and scour the entire building (shop floor, back stairs, stock room etc) for boxes to bale, thus avoiding a build-up at the end of the day. However, this wasn't always a good idea as by the time I'd returned from my reconnaissance trip there would be a gargantuan build-up of boxes back in the baling room.

There was one particular stockroom porter called Kevin Chadbolt who spent a good deal of time reading the paper in the staff toilet. He was a cheerful, cheeky, rebellious and quite tough sort of gentleman who liked to get one over on the establishment.

He also liked sabotage.

Very occasionally, usually on a Friday, he would burst into my baling room and insert a screwdriver into an important looking part of the machine, completely disabling it.

SPIKE WEBB

"There you are that's fucked them. You'll have an easy day now mate!"

Then he'd leave, laughing as he went.

On the one hand I felt chuffed that I had been included in this sense of mischief and camaraderie, grateful even that he had wanted to improve things for me. Yet on the other I was exasperated. Far from making my day easier, he had succeeded in guaranteeing it to be a lot harder as no matter how long it took for the machine to be put back into working order, the boxes still had to be baled by the end of the day.

And they kept coming thick and fast.

However, during my three months at BHS, I can honestly say I left that baling room clear of cardboard every evening. By the time I left I had completely mastered the art of box destruction and cardboard disposal.

I had become a professional baler.

And to this day, I maintain the very same approach to the domestic disposal of cardboard boxes. Whenever such items need to be dealt with, you'll find me out the front, next to the big brown recycling bin, jumping, stamping and wrestling with a kind of insane delight that takes me back around 35 years. Passers-by often look on with a kind of resigned sympathy, as if observing the raving antics of a man possessed.

'Never mess with a baler when he's angry.'

STRAY BULLETS

It's period 5 at Gatesbury School and the last lesson of the day. On my cover sheet, I see that the register consists of thirty-two year 10 girls (aged 14 to 15) and they will be studying PE. Instead of a cover folder containing set work, there is a written message on the register sheet 'head on over to PE block'. This usually means that I must meet the students in the main PE classroom and escort them to a pre-designated computer room where they continue with self-assessment course work on the school intranet.

I arrive at the PE block to see their PE teacher waiting outside the female changing rooms with a few girls dressed in full gym slips and general PE gear, presumably waiting for the other girls to emerge. Seeing them thus clad, I assume that they are to be engaged in an active PE lesson. The teacher is also dressed appropriately in anticipation of a good old workout and I'm wondering where I am going to fit into all this, dressed as I am in a dark grey suit complete with heavy overcoat and traditional, hard loafers on my feet. I'm a little relieved as I think there has been a mistake:

'Hi, it looks as though I probably won't be needed here after all…'

'No it's ok, you can join us over at the gym hall, I'm getting them all to play table tennis.'

Fast forward 15 minutes and I am presiding over 32 girls playing table tennis in 8 groups of doubles in a vast hall. Or rather I should say attempting to play, because it seems that none of them have acquired even the basic skills of the game. Ping pong balls are flying all over the place accompanied by much hysterical giggling. It occurs to me that, as ever, this will be down to technology. These people have spent so much of their youth immersed in online activity of infinite variety that opportunities for the likes of table tennis have rarely arisen until now. I remember being able to play the game at about 7 years old in the days before the wonders of the internet.

But regardless of their collective table tennis prowess, the circumstances under which I find myself are bizarre to say the least. An onlooker or bystander would be looking at a large group of teenage girls in gym outfits, engaged in the dispersal and retrieval of ping pong balls, among which is a suited man who looks a bit like Rod Stewart in a long overcoat, pacing up and down like an army officer in charge of a battalion of men. The girls are a little unnerved by my presence, which is understandable as I am clearly not a PE teacher and do not remotely resemble a table tennis coach, even if such a thing exists.

I take a turn over to where the PE teacher is standing, now chatting with someone who I assume is another PE assistant. She is as amused as I am with the situation:

'You look like a prowling lion.'

I recommence my prowling, truly wondering what the point of me being here is. There are two PE supervisors in the gym, both perfectly capable of instructing the girls on the ins and outs of table tennis and who know all the girls fairly well. Why they need a bloke in an old overcoat wandering about as well is beyond me.

What exactly is going to go wrong? I suppose it's possible that there might be some trouble. A fight might break out over a disputed table tennis point that ends up in hair-pulling and even fisticuffs. And we all know what that can lead to. It could escalate into an all-girl battle with flying bats and handbags, tables being pushed over and ear-piercing screams. I'd have to wade in and, in my capacity as Cover Support, sort it all out. I'd become the suited and booted enforcer, or a kind

TAKE COVER!

of in-house Batman, suppressing yet another hissy free-for-all barny in the table tennis hall.

I think not. And even if it did, wading into a bunch of teenage girls having a bundle certainly wouldn't do my reputation any favours. As I'm musing over all this, a ping pong ball hits me on the forehead, which becomes the catalyst for much mirth and giggling. In fact, I turn to see the girl responsible with her hand over her mouth in embarrassment, doubled up with laughter. I laugh as I throw the ball back.

After all, we're all in this game together.

EXTRA PROVISIONS

I'm looking out of the window whilst sat in the bar in the Premier Hotel on Clarendon Road, Watford. I have with me a Guinness, and I'm feeling emotional. Why? Because a year ago I promised myself I would come here and enjoy a moment or so to reflect or even celebrate. At that time I would have been rushing by in the street outside, usually in the rain, the pockets of my ripped and dilapidated puffer jacket stuffed full of partially used toilet rolls.

Let me explain:

Exactly a year preceding this moment I was still working as an evening cleaner (as well as a cover support teacher during the day) in the office toilets a few yards down the road from where I'm sitting. As I've said before, I was doing that because I needed the money to pay for things like bills and beer. So anything extra that helped with household bills was always a plus. There were four adults living at our council house at the time with another couple of people occasionally staying the night, so the pack of eight toilet rolls included in the Saturday weekly shop would often run a bit low as the week progressed, creating the need for a top-up purchase of more toilet rolls to compensate and meet the sanitary needs of the household.

Cut back to that time and I'm in the office toilets at Clarendon Road. I've been told from the start that any partially used toilet rolls should be thrown in the bin, from whence they would presumably disappear into waste oblivion. For a couple

TAKE COVER!

of months I have been doing just that – ripping them off their holders in the closets, with some gusto, especially when my mood is less than relaxed, and throwing them with pleasurable force into the metal toilet bins before replacing them with new ones from vast packs stacked high in the cleaning cupboard.

One evening, it occurs to me that rather than throw the unwanted, partially used toilet rolls away, I could take just a few home each night to top up my household supply. Why not? After all, they are only going to end up re-emerging in some vile landfill cess pit. So I start slipping the odd roll into my trouser pockets which are cargo pants and conveniently quite deep. Nothing much to start with, just a few to see how it goes. A few small ones just a couple of times a night. But soon, I find myself wanting more. I mean it seems such a waste to chuck them in the bin! And it's making a real difference to our bathroom supply at home – the bog roll basket is topping up nicely on a regular basis for free! Of course, the sizes of partially used bog rolls can vary enormously from cubicle to cubicle. Although small to middling ones can slip effortlessly into my trouser pockets, after a while I'm hungry for bigger, more accommodating cast-offs. I discover with some perseverance that I can get a more substantially sized roll in if I squeeze it first, flattening it just slightly, which is fine because once it's placed in its rightful place in my wicker toilet roll basket at home it can re-expand in due course.

But I am acutely aware that it probably doesn't look very good if you get caught stuffing half used bog rolls down your trouser pockets by your cleaning boss or, worse still, a member of office staff. Not only is it probably against the rules, it's potentially very embarrassing, and I do have some pride. So my bog roll lifting must remain covert at all times. I have discovered the best time to get the biggest catches is around 6.10, the beginning of the evening cleaning shift when all the other cleaners have collected what they need from the cleaning cupboard in the ladies and are busying themselves elsewhere in the building. Naturally, I need to look out for office staff who have a somewhat annoying habit of using the toilets well into the evening. So, there I am, looking furtively up and down the corridor to make sure the coast is clear before shoving another big one into my trousers.

One evening, I tentatively mention to Fizz, my cleaning supervisor, what a waste it seems to be throwing the toilet rolls away as we could probably all do with top-ups at home, to which she responds with absolute conviction that such acts are totally unacceptable to the cleaning company and especially the firm for which we clean and indeed constitutes property theft. The vehemence with which she articulates these sentiments is unexpectedly strong from one who likes to eat her supper in the toilets themselves, but hey, I'm the bad guy here. I quickly drop the subject, but realising that I may have raised a certain amount of suspicion on her part, I resolve to be even more careful when committing my hateful and wanton crime.

The trouble is, my used bog roll theft has become a kind of obsession, an addiction even. I have, during the course of my duties, discovered that I can fit even more substantially sized bog rolls into my puffer jacket pockets. This hangs in the main cleaner's office on the reception area among other cleaners' overcoats, bags and scarves etc. It's right out in the open and in full view of anyone in that area. However, there are no reception staff as they've gone home, so I only need to avoid late night workers nipping to the loo and, of course, my fellow cleaners, in particular Fizz the supervisor.

To get a large toilet roll from the toilets to that little cleaner's cloakroom is no mean feat, because the contraband has to be transported in my trousers across reception and then transferred very quickly into my puffa jacket pockets behind closed doors, before anyone comes in to get anything. And, of course, it must be done at the start of the evening's proceedings, leaving my trouser pockets free to accommodate the smaller bog rolls as the shift progresses.

All this furtive sneaking and running about can make a man a bit nervous. On one occasion, it gets very scary. I'm replacing the used bog rolls in the ladies, my first call of duty on a Tuesday evening. I'm aware that it's only the beginning of the week and already our recently replenished supply at home has dwindled alarmingly quickly, and I'm determined to rectify

TAKE COVER!

this situation with some stealthy work on tonight's shift. I've already hidden a few small to medium sized rolls behind some big boxes containing sanitary gloves in the cleaning cupboard to slip into my trousers later. My mission now is to stuff some bigger sized rolls into those pockets, one in each trouser leg, and somehow get them into my puffer jacket pockets in the cleaners' cloakroom in reception. I look down the main toilets corridor that leads through a series of fire doors onto the upstairs landing which runs adjacent to an open plan office (with a few straggler staff still working late), and thence down a winding staircase and out onto the main reception area, in which is the cleaner's office and cloakroom, and my big puffa jacket. The coast down the corridor is clear so I decide to go for it, but as I'm about to leave the ladies, I spy a nice big bog roll that's been placed on the municipal bin. It's only seen a bit of use, about three quarter full size. Now that really would be a waste, and imagine if I could stuff that big baby into the ample space in my inside puffer jacket pocket as well! I can't resist it, so I snap it up. I'll carry it down to the cloakroom. I know it's real risky but hey, just this once and never again.

But I know I've got to be quick, so I march forcefully down the corridor, determined. After all, it won't matter if an office staff member sees a cleaner carrying a virtually unused toilet roll around with him. What's so unusual about that? I mean, I'm a cleaner right? I could be off to sort out some problem in any number of toilets, it's simply not going to bother them. They've got far better things to be thinking about; finance reports, spreadsheets, business plans, meetings. Cleaners carry brooms, cloths, sprays and vacuum cleaners called Henry around all the time, why not a toilet roll? It's Fizz and the rest of the team I have to watch out for. The important thing is to look as though I'm on business, not too furtive. However I've only gone a few yards when I hear one of the outer fire doors burst open, so I quickly dart into the Mens. Of course, I don't know who or why that person is heading down the corridor, so I slip into trap one and wait. I can hear a familiar hum and realise it's Fizz herself, probably on her way into the Ladies, either to fetch something or to prepare her supper (as mentioned before she likes to dine in the toilets – usually a light pasta salad featuring boiled egg and tuna), so I figure I can make a run for it.

I leave the cubicle and look out into the corridor. Empty, good. I run then slow to a brisk walk as I hear Fizz re-enter the corridor behind me. I'm holding the loo roll in front of me so she can't see it, but it's clear I'm holding something. I manage to get through the two sets of fire doors and out onto the landing, where to my dismay are three office staff discussing something. My earlier assumptions still intact, I stroll confidently past them towards the stairs, nodding politely as I go. Just as I'm thinking that was a breeze one of them glances at my loo roll and I'm convinced he frowned. Oh no, what if they were discussing cleaning/admin costs and waste cutting policies? And Fizz is on my tail too.

I can't go back, so it's all about speed now. I'm taking the stairs down to reception two-by-two. Once more to my dismay, Eva the Swedish desk polisher and Fizz's smoking pal is coming up as I turn the corner to the bottom set of stairs and I almost knock her flying. She looks at me and my bog roll quizzically, raising her eyebrows. I have to say something as I hurry by.

'Sorry Eva, just got one for the basin in the office!'

She looks confused. I don't blame her. What on earth does that mean? One for the basin? The cleaners' office and cloakroom doesn't even have a basin, and even if it did, why would it need a toilet roll?

I figure it's time to abort my mission and loose the bog roll in the downstairs toilets. But as I step onto the shiny reception floor at the foot of the stairs, I slip in some spillage. Picking myself up, Eva seems concerned.

'Yoo Oh kay?'

'Yes, thanks Eva, just been in a bit of a hurry – a bit behind tonight…'

'Oh Kay – tayke it eeeasy – don won fall over ha! Ha!'

I laugh in appreciation, throw the loo roll up and catch it in gay abandon to emphasise my sense of self-ridicule, thus deflecting any suggestion that I might have been attempting to

TAKE COVER!

steal it and then saunter off through the lower fire doors and into the downstairs toilets, without even glancing at the cleaners' cloakroom.

Fizz is probably right behind me so I decide to make for the Mens until the coast is clear. But as I get half way down the corridor Fizz calls from behind.

'Spike – can I have a word?'

As she approaches I'm thinking this is it, I've been rumbled. I'm going to get done for attempting to steal partially used toilet rolls. I'm a little shaky.

'Y – yes? Everything ok?'

'There's been a complaint.'

'Oh – what's that?'

'There's some crap all over the skirting boards in the upstairs Mens cubicle number three – been there all day apparently – can you make sure you scrub it away when you're mopping the floors later?'

I can hardly contain my relief.

'Fantastic! Sure, yeah of course – no problem, it'll be a pleasure!'

'Ok, thanks Spike.'

Fizz looks a bit surprised at my enthusiasm, which is understandable. I'm sure few people have ever expressed such joy at receiving such an instruction. I might as well have suggested celebrating with a glass of bubbly after work.

So the good news is they're not onto me after all. As Fizz goes back upstairs, I'm thinking I'm still holding that bog roll and she didn't even notice. It's now or never so I open the fire doors and look out into reception and over at the door to the cloakroom, which is about ten yards away. Through the windows in the double doors next to it I can see someone's busy polishing desks, but no-one else is around. All is quiet, no-one's coming.

I make a dash for it. As I'm closing the cloakroom door behind me before depositing the bog roll in the inside pocket of my puffa jacket, I hear the main reception door open. I'd better be quick, here goes. I start stuffing the roll into the inside pocket. Trouble is, it's a bit too big and I'm having a problem getting it right in. I can hear someone approaching across the reception. What now? Cleaners hurriedly stuffing things into their pockets mid-shift definitely doesn't look good. If I'm caught my defence could hardly be that I was doing it for my family. I manage to get it mostly in as the door opens. I make an elaborate show of patting my puffa jacket down in the manner of one who has successfully hung it on the coat rack and rested it efficiently in its rightful place, before looking up to see that it's Karl, the boss of the cleaning company.

Fizz's boss, in fact.

Before he has the chance to ask me what I'm doing in here, I take the initiative.

'I was getting hot in this thing – not the ideal thing to be wearing when you're scrubbing toilets and basins!'

'Yes, well most of our cleaners tend to leave their coats behind at the beginning of the shift.'

And as we both walk back out into reception:

'Yes, I normally do but it was a bit nippy earlier so I kept mine on.'

Karl looks a bit confused, probably because whenever he's popped in before I've always been covered in sweat, wearing as little as possible. In fact, the standard branded company T-shirt I am required to wear usually has dark patches of sweat all over it. I tend to look like someone who has never been cold in his life. Changing the subject, Karl tells me he'd like some help carrying some supplies to replenish the stock in the cleaning cupboard and store rooms. He's just delivered them outside the main doors at reception. I go with him and allow myself an inward smile as we begin carrying huge multi-packs of fresh toilet rolls back into the building.

Fast forward again to one year later and I'm sitting with my Guinness, as I promised myself, musing over my life as a part time cleaner. In the western world, where relative luxury abounds, which means working for a reasonable living, spending money on moderate recreation and having a couple of holidays a year is the norm; stealing bog rolls from the toilets that you clean for a living is about as low as it gets. But it's great fun. At one point, I remember thinking to myself, hang on

TAKE COVER!

– I was a copywriter in advertising being taken to lunch a lot, choosing the best of deluxe dining and opting for the finest wines while making TV commercials in London. And now this? Oh well, shit happens.

And thank fuck for that.

FRIENDLY FIRE

It's mid-afternoon and I have a day off from cover teaching as I wasn't called by the agency this morning. To try and secure some more work, I've been spending spare hours every now and then delivering my own leaflets around my hometown, advertising my services as a freelance English language teacher. I've been hoping that some of the posher roads might house au pairs, foreign exchange workers desperate to improve their English. To date, I must have delivered over two thousand flyers with not one response. I realise it's approaching the end of the spring term, so the cover support work will dry up for a while. And anyway, I can't rely on that indefinitely. So I'm feeling a bit heavy hearted, downtrodden as I remember with fondness my working life as a copywriter in London.

Then my mobile phone rings.
'Hello?'
'Eyloh?'
'Who is this?'
'I no speak Eeenglish!'
'really?'
'I won learn!'

I'm feeling a little encouraged as this could be the first response to my leaflets.
'You teach me?'
'Certainly, where do you…'
'How much?'
'Er…'

TAKE COVER!

'How much for me learn Eeenglish?'

'I'd really need to take some details...'

'I won learn! You teacher huh?!'

I'm getting suspicious now as I can hear stifled laughter in the background. Then his voice changes to an American gangster-type accent.

'Come on buddy how much we talkin?'

I decide to play along.

'I charge thirty pounds an hour.'

'Thirty bucks?'

'That's right, thirty pounds.'

'Thirty bucks to learn your dumb language? Get outa here!'

'Ok, I'll wipe that stupid accent off your face for twenty.'

'Call it a fiver buddy and you got yourself a deal!'

'I'm a bit busy so I really have to go now.'

And with that, I hang up. But I'm laughing because it was genuinely very funny. In fact, part of me wanted to ring back, find out where they lived and go round for a good old laugh, but I don't think that was their intention. I'm also feeling more than a bit down, because I've been mocked when all I'm trying to do is make a living, all be it doing stuff I don't particularly want to do. Soon I'll be off to clean up other people's mess which is never an exciting proposition. But I can't complain, because I consider myself lucky even to have that option.

Then I'm reminded of some considerable instances of uncanny good fortune that I was lucky enough to be the recipient of when I had proper jobs as a younger man...

FLASHBACK: LUCKY BREAKS — THE CIVIL SERVICE

The Civil Service Department of Employment Head Quarters, Reed's School, Orphanage Road, Watford. A vast, Victorian building of gargantuan proportions that loomed mysteriously behind the tracks at Watford Junction Station. Its central beacon was a tall clock tower with a huge clock face that told the wrong time to all who glanced at it from miles around. The structure was originally built to accommodate many of London's orphans in the mid-nineteenth century and was known as Reed School London Orphanage. During World War Two, the orphans were evacuated (dispersed up and down the country presumably) and it became a prisoner of war hospital, after which it was commandeered by the Department of Employment and thereafter used as government offices – Civil Service Headquarters for the DE.

So it was in this haunted place, full of pen-pushing Civil Servants and ghostly lost souls, that I was to spend the next ten and a half years earning a minimal salary at minimal hours in order to concentrate on becoming a rock star. I joined the department in February 1978 because the singer in my band Sid Sideboard and The Chairs also worked there and told me about the advantages of the work attendance scheme called 'flexi-time'. You could arrive anytime between 8 and 10, take

TAKE COVER!

up to two hours lunch between 12 and 2pm (minimum of 30 mins) and leave anytime between 4 and 6. The idea was to make sure you worked for a total of 37 hours a week, which worked out at an average of seven hours twelve minutes a day. You could carry over a maximum of ten hours credit or deficit each month. You filled in your own times, each day, on a 'flexi-sheet.' These sheets would be checked and signed off by your Executive Officer (line manager) at the end of each week or month depending on how important they felt the whole thing was.

Most of the elderly civil servants tended to build up flexi-time credit because it meant that they could use it to take extra days off, known as 'flexi days'. Younger people like myself, however, tended to be less pragmatic about the situation in the long term and were more inclined to use the scheme to our advantage on a more daily basis. This often meant coming into work at 10 in the morning, taking two hours for a liquid lunch and going home at 4 o clock.

Many people tended to be a little if not considerably creative when filling in their flexi-sheets, depending on how often their EO's checked them and how fastidious they were about it. It was really a question of how good you were at fooling everyone in the office. Massaging your attendance hours was known as 'fiddling your flexi', and if you were caught, it was technically a case of instant dismissal and considered to be a criminal offence, as you were 'stealing time' from the government (although nobody ever implemented these measures as it would make them seem inefficient as managers).

One good way to fiddle your flexi was to wait until everyone had left the office (usually 8 to 10 people) at say, 5.20 in the afternoon, give it five minutes and leave at 5.25 and enter 6 o'clock on your flexi-sheet. Or, if you were the first one in at 8.45, you would enter 8 o'clock on your flexi-sheet. Lunchtimes were not as easy as a lot of people (especially the older ones) tended to eat sandwiches at their desks for half an hour and build up flexi that way.

The scheme was originally introduced by the Civil Service Department Heads as a way of easing the pressure on clerical officers whose desk jobs were usually incredibly boring, depending on which department you worked in. Over my ten and a half years in the Civil Service I moved from department to department, from one side of the complex to the other. Some positions I occupied were vaguely tiresome with moments of random interest, others were so hideously tedious that they could propel a young man in his twenties to the outskirts of insanity and firmly on the road to madness. These were the times when my flexi-time management was most inventive and skilful.

Then, one day, the game was up.

Probably the most boring job I had in the Civil Service was the manual unemployment count in the Statistics Department (Stats C1) in 1982. That meant me and one other person counting the number of unemployed people in England, Wales and Scotland. Every benefit office and careers office in every town submitted monthly sheets on which were listed hand written figures for unemployed persons looking for work in four categories: male, female, full time, part time. These forms were also divided into ten Standard Regions: North, North West, Yorkshire and Humberside, West Midlands, East Midlands, East Anglia, South West, South East, Wales and Scotland. The forms came in batches of different colours, depending on the region. My job was to check that the 'total' numbers for each category had been calculated correctly by the clerical officer at the benefit/careers office. I would then enter those four total figures from each form onto a huge table before using a large manual calculator to add all the numbers up to produce an accumulated total for each Standard Region.

And I was supposed to be becoming a rock star.

I couldn't really fiddle my flexi as I was in a small room with no windows and only two other people sitting opposite me, one of whom was my Executive Officer and boss (Valerie Parsons – a very sweet lady). So I simply spent lots of time away from the office but told the truth on my flexi sheet, ending up owing hours and then days to the department.

My work output was dreadful, sometimes verging on nil. My superiors were surprisingly understanding, but

TAKE COVER!

nonetheless frustrated. Fortunately, the official unemployment statistical count had been recently moved onto a computer software system called JUVOS and the manual count was kept on for a while to run alongside it as an experiment to see how the two compared in accuracy. But if someone like me refused to do it properly it all became a bit pointless, which arguably it was in the first place. My attitude was not helped by the fact that my girlfriend of three years had just gone off to university in Windsor and I was scared of her finding someone else, which of course she did, as is commonplace when girls are nineteen and starting out in life.

However, during my time in this particular office I managed to behave so disgracefully that I was divested of the flexi-time privilege and put onto standard 'chartered' hours as a punishment until I paid back all the hours I owed from not being in the office very much. Being in my early twenties, I failed to appreciate that no matter how boring something is, if you're being paid to do it you should actually do it. Or go away and let someone else have the job. And girlfriends going to university does not even feature in the rule book.

After a year or so of this I was transferred into the next office, Stats C2, which was where I was charged to provide written answers to parliamentary questions and statistical information asked for in the House of Commons on a daily basis. This was known as the PQ section. This was far more interesting and the office was bigger, lighter with some windows and sometimes I actually enjoyed being there. I had been put back on flexi-time but was still, however, naughty with my time-keeping.

Nonetheless, after a while in the PQ section and then in a public enquiries statistical department, I began to feel a real need to move on. I still had ambitions to be a rock star of some kind and was playing in bands, rehearsing laboriously once a week in various horrible practise studios with other equally unwilling musicians in their mid-twenties. But part of me was beginning to realise that there was a vague possibility that, however good a drummer I may be, I might not be behaving in a way that makes a person likely to become a pop star. Going to the civil service every day and then the pub most evenings may not bring that top agent knocking on the band's collective door.

And as luck would have it, one day, completely out of the blue, I got a phone call at work from a friend who was working in advertising. Would I like to leave the civil service and go and work as a copywriter at Saatchi & Saatchi Advertising? No CV required and no interview. Just walk straight into a new career making up adverts at one of the world's most famous and revered advertising agencies.

Nice one. If I had bothered to go to Sheffield university to study English Literature and graduated with a good degree, I wouldn't have been able to get near the door of an agency of that calibre or repute. Most post graduates worked their way up in small, out of town agencies, only dreaming of one day getting into a major London outfit. Yet cheeky old me just spends ten years messing around in the civil service doing very little and then bags the dream job just when he's had enough farting about.

It also turned out that some of my other close friends (also musicians) had been working in the same Saatchi offices for a while and would be able to show me the ropes. So there was no nervous anticipation, just a golden opportunity to change direction into something very exciting.

Most people would say that this particular instance of good fortune would likely be my quota career-wise. But not so. After six years working at Saatchi & Saatchi in London's Charlotte Street, something really uncanny happened.

BOLT OUT OF THE BLUE

Summer 1994. Watford Junction Station, platform 7. I should really have been on platform 9 to catch the Silverlink train into Euston as my ticket wasn't strictly valid for the faster Intercity service from platform 7. Still, lots of people did it. I mean, it's the same journey right? And usually nobody said anything.

Soon I was sitting comfortably, quietly contemplating the day ahead at Saatchi & Saatchi writing copy for Dixons press ads; the usual set of layouts to fit words to, mainly product descriptors and pricing detail. It was a bit boring really, cutting and pasting previous ads and editing according to media size and layout design. As usual, I took out my novel and started to read. I was interrupted by a voice opposite.

'I see we're both on the naughty train again.'

I looked up and recognised a very tall black man with a big smile on his face. We'd been nodding to each other on the platform on the odd occasion. I was feeling in a good mood so I decided to close my book and enter into conversation. It turned out that the gentleman opposite was in marketing but was also a part time actor and had featured in a TV commercial for 'Millar Lite'. I mentioned that I was in advertising, working as a copywriter on retail accounts for Saatchi & Saatchi.

'Do you enjoy what you do?'

'Yes, it's only retail, you know, straight forward press ads for Dixons, but it suits me down to the ground as you can plan your day easily and there's no hanging around after work trying to crack difficult briefs for flash accounts like Toyota…'

I explained that I was also a drummer and often needed to get away on time for gigs or rehearsals.

Then a voice piped up from across the gangway.

'Excuse me, do you mind if we interrupt?'

I looked across to see three men sitting at a table.

'Not at all…'

'Would you like to come and work at Thompsons?'

'What…you mean J Walter Thompson?'

'Yeah, we've just won the 54 million pound Boots account and we've got no one to work on it!'

'Really?'

'Problem is, JWT don't really do retail and everyone in the creative department is refusing to touch it. You've just talked yourself into a job. By the way, I'm Mike Murphy and this is Mark Wilkins, we're group heads and we've been asked to find a creative team to take it on. This is our friend from Grey. Strangely enough, we asked him earlier if he knew anyone and he said he didn't – and then you came on and started talking!'

Soon everyone was on the concourse at Euston shaking hands. It was arranged for my art director, Gary, and I to meet them at their office at JWT the next morning.

I told Gary as soon as I got into the office and he said we'd better get down there and see what was on offer. The problem was that although J Walter Thompson are one of the best advertising agencies, Saatchi & Saatchi were the most renowned in those days and the work we did on Dixons was fairly secure. We were earning around 23k a year which was not at all bad in 1994. I asked another creative director friend what we should ask for salary wise and he said go for 35k.

'Why not? They are clearly in a tight spot and don't have a clue what you earn!'

So next day Gary and I found ourselves sitting in Mike and Mark's office at JWT on leafy Berkeley Square. They had their feet up on their desks and were strumming stratocaster

TAKE COVER!

electric guitars, jamming together through a couple of practice amps.

'So guys, what do you reckon on coming in and working on Boots?'

It had been decided that I would do the talking.

'Well, although we're quite comfortable at Saatchi's, this seems like a real opportunity to...'

'Cut the crap how much do you want?'

'W – well we wouldn't really consider moving for any less than 35k...'

'How does 40 sound?'

'S – sounds fine. Er...can we go away and think about it?'

Sure guys no problem – give us a ring later on.'

Gary and I kept our composure until we were in the lift when we exclaimed in unison:

'Forty f****** grand!'

Back at Saatchi's, our friends and colleagues were naturally pleased for us and advised us to make the most of the situation by asking for other benefits before agreeing to take up the position.

So I rang Mike Murphy at JWT:

'We're happy with the salary, but could we also possibly have a car each?'

He said he'd get back to me. In the meantime, though, someone pointed out to us that having a company car is actually a bad idea as you get taxed higher. So when Mike rang back:

'Yeah a car's no problem...'

'Thanks but actually we'd prefer not to have a car – can we just have some more money?'

'Ok I'll find out.'

Later he rang back and said we can have another 5k each.

'Thanks that's great. One last thing though. As you know, we'll have to give Saatchi's a month's notice, after which we'd both like to go on holiday for a week...so we were thinking, as well as our five weeks yearly holiday, can we also have a week's extra holiday on full pay before we start?'

SPIKE WEBB

That doesn't seem to be a problem either.

So, in the space of a couple of days I had virtually doubled my salary and was about to have an easy time of it working a month's notice at Saatchi's before going on a week's extra holiday on full pay at my next job.

And all because of a conversation on a train.

Of course, Gary and I were a little apprehensive with regard to how hard we might be required to work for our 40 grand. But we needn't have worried. On eventually starting at JWT, we discovered our lives were to be even more comfortable than expected.

It was our first day at JWT and we arrived promptly in reception at 9 o'clock. We waited a little nervously for a short while until a very pleasant young lady introduced herself and showed us to our office on the creative floor. She said to make ourselves comfortable and that 'Graham from traffic' would be along to see us soon.

For those who don't know, the 'traffic' department is responsible for directing and monitoring the allocation and progress of work in the creative department. Graham was responsible for the progress of the new Boots brief, on which we would be working.

So we got ourselves a coffee from a free machine down the corridor and waited for about an hour. Then came a knock on our door and in walked a very relaxed, smiling chap who introduced himself as Graham.

'Boy are we glad to see you guys.'

'Really?'

'Yeah, we've had the Boots account for a few weeks and this last week the client's been on at us to get some ads done. So I'm afraid I've got an apology…'

'Oh really?'

'Really sorry, I know it's a bit out of order, but we need to ask you to do an ad!'

'Oh well, don't worry, that's kind of why we're here.'

'But on your first day? It's a bit of a cheek really. It's only a small 25 x 4 press ad. When would be convenient for someone to come down and talk to you about it?'

TAKE COVER!

'Well, er, anytime.'

'Thanks, really appreciate it.'

After some more pleasantries, Graham left our office and shortly after we received a call from the Boots account girl:

'When would it be convenient to come and brief you guys?'

'About half an hour?'

'Ahh, that's great thanks so much!'

Half an hour later we were briefed on a small press ad for 'Wash n Go' shampoo now 3 for 2 at Boots. The copy (words, my department) comprised pricing details and a phrase:

'Subject to availability' in small writing at the bottom of the ad.

I didn't want anyone to think I didn't care, so I questioned the need for that phrase. They thanked me for my concern but explained it was a legal requirement.

Well, at least I'd done some work, and after about ten minutes Gary finished the layout so we went to lunch. After wandering around for a while we came across a pub called The Running Footman, a traditional London Pub set deep in the leafy backstreets just off Berkeley Square in the heart of London's Mayfair. Very nice.

We had a pint and a sandwich. A bit pricey, but hey, this was Mayfair and we could afford it on what we were earning. Then in walked Mike Murphy, our senior art director and group head. Our boss, in fact.

'Hi guys, thought I might find you in one of our locals round here. Welcome aboard! The brief is you do exactly what you want.'

'Pardon?'

'We like our people to enjoy themselves at JWT. So as long as your work is of a high standard and you meet the deadlines, there are no rules. If you're not busy, there's no need to hang around the agency – just have a good time.'

'Great, thanks.'

'Have you eaten?'

'We had a sandwich...' 'That's not a proper lunch, come on I'll buy you a bowl of pasta.'

SPIKE WEBB

So we ended up in a very nice Italian restaurant just round the corner, enjoying traditional pasta with fine wine before returning to the office at around 3.30 pm.

The Boots ad that we had prepared earlier was still on Gary's desk so I rang Graham to let him know it was ready.

'That's great, thanks very much. I'll tell Mandy it's ready for collection.'

Shortly after Mandy rang and we arranged a convenient time for her to come and fetch the ad, take it away to check with her colleagues and send it to production, after which a laminated copy would be despatched to us for our approval before going to press.

Later that afternoon, Graham came to see us.

'Boy has word got around about you.'

'Really?'

'Not only doing an ad on your first day but so quickly and efficiently!'

"Well it was nothing really."

Our lives at JWT continued to be most enjoyable over the next three and a half years. We went on to work on TV commercials, go to the advert shoots, post production and hang out with producers and directors, enjoying expensive, extended lunches, chauffeur-driven cars and all kinds of other benefits.

Then, one morning, Gary and I were summoned to the creative director's office.

'Sit down guys! Sorry, bad news I'm afraid. Martin Sorrell at WPP has asked me to lose a hundred grand from my creative department. You two add up to that, so I'm having to make you redundant. It's no reflection on your ability – you're a good creative team. It's purely fiscal.

'We've put together a good package; eighteen grand each plus any holiday pay you're owed.'

We were jointly surprised and of course dismayed. Gutted even. We loved our job, and it paid very well. Having said that, eighteen grand was a lot of money in 1997 and a nice little nest egg of savings – assuming we could get another job fairly quickly, which as relatively young men was quite likely.

TAKE COVER!

We went back to our office to start putting our portfolio together. Shortly after the chief account girl on Boots walked in, eagerly carrying a pile of press and TV requests to brief us on.

'Sorry, can't touch those.'
'What do you mean?'
'We're outa here – just been made redundant.'
'But who's going to do this lot – we've promised the Boots client scripts and ads by the end of the week.'
'Well, we did wonder how you would cope with that particular dilemma.'

She said she'd have to take her director in charge and see the creative director to explain that there was no-one else in the creative department to do the work. Two days later we were back in the office working in exactly the same job as freelancers on a higher daily rate than our salary had paid us – plus, we got to keep all the redundancy money.

When it rains it really does pour.

PLOTTING CO-ORDINATES

Thursday afternoon, Leaton Down School. I'm in a very large science room, adorned with long benches that run side to side down the middle of the room. The students have been relocated here to study mathematics. All seven of them. Year tens. So the room is sparsely populated to say the least, which makes my being here even more like a kind of elephant in the room, because we all know there's no need for me to be there at all. I can't teach mathematics, and even if I could, I wouldn't be qualified to attempt GCSE level. This is made even more ridiculous when I find out what it is I must ask them to do.

I am to give them each a sheet of squares with a list of co-ordinates which they must plot and connect, the successful outcome of which will reveal a picture graphic in all its glory.

These people are roughly fifteen years old. OK, so the reason there are only seven of them is likely to be that they are very poor students who have little hope of passing any GCSE exams, and they probably hold more mainstream students back because they are simply not interested. But we have to continue with this charade as I wander up and down, magnanimously placing the sheets in front of them as though distributing some kind of mid-afternoon snack. Some look bored and miserable as they begin the exercise, others chat quietly as they do it.

But being young adults will mean they know some of the basics to greater or lesser degrees; a little maths perhaps,

TAKE COVER!

some English. They can count, and they can speak and write things down.

They also know a thing or two about life; girls, boys, football, music, parties, money and the need to earn it, and a lot of other stuff. So why insult them by asking them to spend an hour of their lives doing what amounts to little more than joining up some big dots to reveal an infantile image that a three-year-old might possibly be impressed with?

But they are resigned to it. In fact, they are doing the task without really thinking about it, chatting as they go. I stroll up and down aimlessly, occasionally looking over a shoulder to feign interest in what the image will turn out to be.

'I wonder what it is. You're getting there – it looks like an animal of some kind.'

But they know that I know that the whole thing is a complete farce. How could any of us possibly be interested in the outcome of this infantile process? As such I really am the elephant in the room. The personification of all that is absurd about providing cover support teaching for a few harmless near-adults who have simply been fobbed off for an hour because they will never amount to anything academically.

They know it, and I know it.

After a while, one lad calls me over to show me a photo of a bike he is in the process of painting with a friend. He tells me they are also doing up an old motorbike, retro style. They intend to sell it. I'm enthused for him.

'You could start up a business eventually.'

He nods enthusiastically.

'Yes Sir, that's what we're going to do, the plan is to go into business together!'

I'm flattered he wants to tell me about it, and pleased he wants to share his interest in the painting/mechanic thing.

And what good will those co-ordinates on that sheet of paper ever be to him? But he's happy to carry on doing some, just to please me.

After what seems like an age we reach the end of the lesson and the bell goes to signify the end of our charade. And the image revealed after successful co-ordination of dots and lines?

An elephant.

BATTLE TACTICS

I've learned quite a bit since going back to school. In spite of all the seemingly impossible difficulties to overcome; the fact that most students inevitably see cover periods as a free period and celebrate accordingly, and the restrictions put upon those charged with task of convincing them otherwise, there are some occasions when adopting a different approach can actually work. At the ages of fourteen and fifteen, many people respond very well to a little playful irony. If they have discovered something silly or random to do, relating it with over-exaggerated interest often goes down well.

    I'm at Gatesbury covering a year 9 afternoon lesson in English Language. I've already had an unusual moment with one of the students outside the classroom as they queue before entering. A boy started asking questions in a foreign language. It turned out that he was asking 'How are you, Sir?' in Italian. He proudly proclaimed that he was actually Italian and was by-lingual. However, if it was true, why would he still be raving about it? Anyhow, I knew he would be one to watch over the following fifty minutes.

    The students are to use their textbooks to answer questions relating to some images displayed at the front on a large computer screen. The lesson theme is based on their understanding of irony and its uses in written and spoken language. So, I can answer any questions backed by my knowledge and understanding of the concept.

SPIKE WEBB

As ever, the problem is that very few are interested. They are quite friendly though, not troublemakers. They're very lively and I know I'll need to work hard to keep the chat levels down. I look over at four boys huddling over something in the corner. On moving closer I see that they are fixing together a Star Wars character from a box kit, a bit like the old air fix models but without any glue. Strictly speaking, I should tell them to put it away as the lesson has begun. But they look like they're probably quite boisterous when they are not thus occupied, and it might be better for my sanity over the next forty-five minutes to let them carry on. So, I decide on a kind of compromise.

I approach with their textbooks:

'That looks interesting!'

'Yes, Sir. It's quite difficult to put it together. In fact, it helps us concentrate in class. It's good for our minds.'

'Ahh yes. I can see how this activity must be good therapy for reducing stress levels – so that you can work more effectively.'

'Absolutely, Sir.'

'Tell you what, how about we combine what you're doing with schoolwork, so we get the best results from the lesson? You continue building the Star Wars character whilst occasionally opening your books to look at some work, when you feel refreshed enough?'

They are very approving of this. They heartily agree saying that this was their precise intention:

'Absolutely Sir, that's a very good idea and exactly what we were going to do.'

'So, we have a deal then?'

'Certainly, Sir!'

I move round to a bunch of people at the other side of the room. They are seated at their desks but turning around to chat noisily with each other. I decide to engage in a particularly noisy girl in conversation:

'Do you have many cover lessons?'

'Quite a few, Sir – several every week.'

'Do you think that's too many?'

TAKE COVER!

'Yes – but we wish our science teacher would be off sometimes. He's the one teacher we don't like and the only one who's always here!'

'So you like your English teacher?'

'Yes, she's alright.'

Just as I turn away and walk back to the front desk, I notice something at the back of the class on the far left. The would-be Italian is lying on the floor with his legs up against the wall in a vertical position.

I approach:

'That's an Interesting posture.'

'Thank you, Sir. I'm doing this because I have a rare spinal condition. It's important for me to do these stretching exercises to make it better, Sir.'

Yes, I see. I also know about this rare spinal condition because I'm actually a medical practitioner. I only do this cover teaching for pure enjoyment. There's something else about this condition which I'm sure you've been told about.'

'What's that, Sir?'

'It's also important to sit straight in your chair immediately after the exercise has been completed in order to balance the activity and natural tensions in your back.'

'Yes, you're right Sir, I was just about to sit back in the chair.'

And with that he sits back at his desk.

The rest of the lesson continues with pockets of relatively harmless incidents, with me having to quieten things down at regular intervals. About ten minutes before the end I go over to the model makers to see how they're getting on. It turns out they've just finished successfully assembling the Start Wars character and are engaged in operating its gun firing feature when I remind them that we had a deal. To my surprise, without remonstration they happily open their books and start discussing the work. I even get a fist greeting from the ringleader and there's no trouble from them during the entire lesson.

Some students have been working all through the lesson despite the background noise made by those who have shown either a passing or absolutely no interest. If the four model makers had been told to stop, chances are they would have been a major problem and possibly succeeded in disrupting proceedings to such an extent that those few who did want to work simply wouldn't have been able to.

Some cover lesson periods are definitely workable, stressful though that still is. But addressing those is all about tactics; unlike some periods, in which the deployment of this kind of tactic is simply futile.

THAT'S QUITE ENOUGH THANK YOU

I'm sitting in a Wetherspoons pub, reading the paper and doing the crossword before making my way for a six o'clock start at my evening cleaning job. There are some quite lively younger people sitting at a table nearby, and occasionally the tranquil murmur of pub conversation is interrupted by bursts of laughter. The strange thing is, I have an almost unconscious urge to go over and reprimand them.

'Er, thank you – that's quite enough – can we keep it down please?'

Of course, in a split second I stop myself as I return to reality, but the urge is very real. I used to be fairly relaxed after a day's work in the office – sitting quietly in a busy pub reading the paper and watching the world go by, but now I'm really jumpy. The subconscious desire for quiet is quite extraordinary. Even as a drummer, I'm used to random loud noises, but now I have a compulsion to quash any sudden sound. A glass banging down on a table, a raised voice, sudden laughter. Sometimes as I'm passing noisy people at the bar, I'm even tempted to interrupt:

'That's quite enough – let's be getting on with the task in hand thank you!'

I've been in the schools a few months now and telling complete strangers to shut up would definitely be a sign that it might be getting to me.

SPIKE WEBB
Better be off to the bogs and do some shit.

NOTHING LIKE A GOOD TUNE TO KEEP YOUR SPIRITS UP

Ten past six on a Monday evening. I'm in the toilets again, having just replaced the loo rolls in the upstairs gents and ladies after a particularly bad day at school. Two cover periods have left me emotionally knackered. As I'm getting stuck into the vanity mirrors, I can't get the vision of those students out of my head.

The first is a bunch of year 8's, who for some reason seem to be verging on the depraved. I can only put it down to hormones. It's late in the summer term, so soon they'll be year 9's, fourteen to fifteen-year-olds. The level of random, uncontrollable behaviour is so extraordinary it is as though they have actually become possessed. I turn to see a group of girls on one table engaged in demented, high pitched giggling, one with water dribbling down her face, wild staring eyes and a look of insane delight on her face.

Attempts to reason with these students are completely futile. I spend some time angrily musing over the fact that they have no idea what awaits them in the real world. I eventually decide to magnanimously announce my decision to let them listen to music on their phones.

'Ok everyone, as it's Friday I've decided to let you listen to music on your mobile phones…'

SPIKE WEBB

This falls against deaf ears, partly because the noise in the room is deafening anyway and also because those who want to listen to music already are. I walk around, trying to appeal to individuals, but they are all literally too far gone. When the bell to indicate lunchtime finally arrives I let out a shattered sigh.

Then, after lunch comes the worst experience I've had in a computer room. It's the last lesson of the day with about fifteen students, mostly male. They have been instructed by their real teacher to use this lesson as a study period (to be presided over by my good self). They must utilise the computers to refresh their knowledge of geographical matters in connection with GCSEs that loom in a couple of years' time. As they all eagerly log on to their large screen, desk top computers, I get the feeling that they're quite keen to brush up on the old geography, and I'm relieved as it looks as though, compared to my last cover lesson, this is going to be a quiet one.

As I'm about to let out a quiet sigh of relief, it starts. The dulcet tones of Rick Astley singing 'Never gonna give you up' fill the room. I clearly can't ignore this, so I move quickly down the centre aisle towards the source of the noise. There's a particularly cheeky student, red in the face, giggling and staring at a screen which is clearly the catalyst of his mirth. As Rick Astley is quickly silenced, I can just about make out a series of colourful icons for selection before he minimizes the display and replaces it with a beautiful image of a rape field.

And as I'm returning to my position:

'Don't you like Rick Astley, Sir?'

'No, so no more of that please.'

I've only been back at my front desk for a few seconds when an aggressive, hard hitting rap track fills the room featuring hostile, racist lyrics. I move quickly toward the same student's desk, but on arrival the rapping has stopped and the screen display is back to its peaceful rape field.

'Let's have less of this nonsense and more concentration on your GCSE work.'

But as I'm making my way back again, 'Never gonna give you up' bellows out from the other side of the room. This

TAKE COVER!

is met with chuckles of laughter as I move quickly over just in time to see another screen of coloured icons disappear. So two students have got onto the same site. Becoming exasperated, I make my way back to the front.

Then comes the sound of Rick Astley again, so I move in the direction of the first offender. As his screen flicks back to normal, the racist rap starts up again from the other side. This continues to raucous student laughter as I rush back and forth like an electronic piggy in the middle. I decide I've had enough.

'Right that's enough!'

'Sorry, Sir!'

I return successfully to my position at the front. There is silence for a while. Then suddenly Rick Astley and the racist rapping fill the room in unison, as I move quickly back toward the computers another sound is put into the mix from another computer. It's that of an extremely provocative male voice, accompanied by a woman screaming in delight. Then the sound of a US gangster shouting, accompanied by gun shots:

'Dance, motherfucker! Dance!

As I run around the room I realise that all the students are sharing the same site, clicking on random coloured buttons, all designed to produce irritating, offensive and even obscene sounds.

The laughter in the room reaches canned audience laughter level as I dart about trying to silence the noise from each computer. The combination of noises is almost surreal:

'Never gonna give you up...grunt...gasp...gunshot...motherfucker...

never gonna give you up...gasp.'

I decide I really have had enough and, resigned, I return to my desk at the front. I have become a target for complete ridicule. These people are intent upon the wanton mockery of a complete stranger. And the most irritating part?

It is funny, and I have become the centrepiece of a slapstick farce. I laugh because that's all there is left to do. Suddenly, all the noises cease and there is nothing but stifled giggling.

SPIKE WEBB

I look at the clock and realise this has been going on for nearly an hour and the bell's about to go. As they all start to get their things together the inevitable happens and 'Never gonna give you up' belts out one last time just as the bell goes.

So I'm not feeling too sprightly in the toilets this evening. Just as I'm spraying the basins with fairly ineffectual cleaning fluid, Fizz bursts in, complete with half-eaten apple in her hand and a can of table polish in the other. She has a message for me.

'There's been a complaint in the cleaner's book.'

'What's that?'

'You're not cleaning the ladies properly.'

'What are they talking about? Properly doesn't mean anything, they need to be more specific.'

Fizz points randomly at some taps and some chrome.

'Those basin taps and the chrome on the soap dispensers need properly cleaning – so that they shine – and the chrome on the waste bins as well.'

She leaves abruptly. She's actually quite nice and doesn't like awkwardness or conflict. I begin to regret my outburst – she was only mentioning something that had been written in the cleaner's comments book by some asshole. She wasn't necessarily in agreement with it. But after a long and stressful day with out-of-control teenagers, you tend to snap sometimes.

As a consequence of this little incident of discourse in the toilets, I set myself a new priority. However frantic my cleaning schedule turns out to be, including special random demands made from time to time on top of my usual duties, I make sure those taps and that chromework shine like they've never shone before, every night. They become my pride and joy.

Later, when I'm kneeling down on a mission to clean a particularly vile toilet in the downstairs Gents, I'm musing over the fact that my reaction to Fizz's comment was a bit like that of a stroppy teenager. I'm giving her a hard time when all she's trying to do is her job – simply because I've had a bad day in school.

TAKE COVER!

But I am being punished, because as I'm vigorously scrubbing a particularly stubborn piece of crap from under the toilet rim, I can't get Rick Astley out of my head.

PRACTICE WHAT YOU PREACH

I'm in one of those moods when I don't care. I'm flossing my teeth wildly down the street on the way to the pub after my cleaning job; spitting out dental debris as I go in full view of anyone who happens to pass, some of whom turn away in a mixture of astonishment and disgust. My next step is to swill round with my miniature mouthwash behind my favourite bush beside the pub wall.

I'm in this kind of mood because after two hours of cleaning up other people's crap, you really don't give a shit. And it's a great feeling. Call it job satisfaction.

And it beats the arse out of being on the dole.

However, it does raise a bit of an issue, considering what I do for a living during the day, albeit temporarily. Providing Cover Support in schools for absent teachers involves the encouragement of good behavior. That is, behaviour that is largely designed not to cause offense to other people, either verbally or visually. If I were to witness a cocky student bowling down the corridor or standing at the back of the class blatantly flossing his/her teeth, gobbing out the stale food for all to see I would be horrified and compelled to try and put a stop to it. Of all the sometimes horrendous things I have witnessed, I have never seen anything as decadent as that. Yet I am happily engaged in such behavior in public when I'm away from the schools.

TAKE COVER!

So that makes me something of a hypocrite.

It's also got me thinking about how teenage students might feel most of the time. My mood was fuelled by having finished something I didn't particularly want to do – but had no real choice under my present circumstances. Similarly, so many schoolkids seem not to want to be at school. They just have to be there. Could it be that their unruly and even anarchic behavior is a result of the same mental process? Whatever the answer, I may have inadvertently answered some of my own questions about why some of these teenagers are so difficult to control.

Time for that pint.

CEASE FIRE

It's mid-morning and I'm on the way to a cover period in the maths block at Gatesbury School during which I shall be presiding over thirty or so year 11s (fifteen/sixteen-year-olds). There are no instructions on my cover sheet as to what they are supposed to be doing and I'm hoping there'll be some information waiting on the teacher's desk. As I enter the classroom, I see that some students have already settled down at their desks. Two big guys at the back have struck an unusual pose. One has his head positioned so that it appears to be growing out of the other's shoulder. What makes this funny is that he has a huge head of thick, curly ginger hair that grows upwards and outwards, like an uncontrollable hedge, and he is grinning insanely. He's clearly in high spirits:

'Morning Sir, are you having a good day?'
'Yes, thank you. That is an interesting posture.'
'Do you like it, Sir?'
'I certainly don't have a problem with it.'
'Thank you, Sir.'

We laugh, normal positions are resumed and our truce has been successfully established, a positive start to the lesson. It turns out that they are supposed to be revising for their maths GCSE exam, and they have the necessary books etc with them. Some start revising, others do not. But at their age and juncture in academic life, there seems little point in me attempting to bully them into maths revision, even if it is one of the more fundamental subjects for inclusion on a CV. I'd rather just get

TAKE COVER!

on with them. From a philosophical point of view, it's becoming increasingly obvious that I am not the right man for the job.

Why? Because I care what they think of me, and actually that should be the last thing on my mind. Presumably, you learn about all these personal juxtapositions when you train to be a teacher, but I've had no training for secondary schools, just foreign learners on a one-month TEFL crash course in London. And anyway, I'm a drummer. I'm only paid slightly more than a cleaner to come in here and watch over these people approaching adulthood.

So does it really matter what I say to them?

One guy is loving his music while he studies. Should I ask him to put his phone away and cause a bit of a scene which would spoil the harmony in the class? That would be disruptive in itself, because some people, those who want to, are working in peace. No-one is being disruptive, so why should I create a problem where there isn't one?

Ok, so there is a problem in that mobile phone use is forbidden in class as a matter of school policy and technically against the rules, but if these people haven't embraced those rules by now, they never will.

The guy with the hedge on his head is chatting quietly, but animatedly with his mate. When I look over, he glances back and nods politely, still with a beaming smile. I wonder what life is like for him. He doesn't seem inclined to revise mathematics, but I get a sense of contentment. He's about to enter the maze of unknown challenges that life will present, yet he's still a happy soul.

The class file out after the bell goes, and I get a final cheeky nod from hedge head before he's off down the corridor, still chatting with his mate. I saunter back to the staff room, genuinely hoping he'll get some luck in life.

After a glance at my cover sheet schedule, I'm delighted to see that I'm free for the next period and then it's lunch, which will be my usual stroll by the open fields whilst chomping secretly on a homemade sandwich.

SPIKE WEBB

After lunch, I'm waiting in an English classroom for the arrival of about ten year 10 students. It's not long before I get the feeling that it's not by any means going to be a quiet affair. I can see some of them approaching across the quads, in particularly high spirits. I recognise some of them and, more to the point, they recognise me.

'Rod!'

Whilst this is flattering and like most people, I like to be liked, it's also unnerving because this room is especially visible to people passing by, in particular proper teachers and members of the school authorities. So appearing to be seemingly lacking control of a class doesn't do your reputation much good. Of course, I'm only assuming this as I don't really know what other cover teachers are like.

There's a bit of a crush as the students surge into the classroom, almost as though they are arriving at a party. They arrange themselves in positions that will afford them the best possible time for the next hour, happy in the knowledge that good old Rod is one who wears such behaviour fairly well. One guy imitates something he's seen me do on a number of occasions at the start of a lesson and raises both arms so that they are stretched out on either side at shoulder level.

Everyone laughs.

I'm a little flattered because he's impersonating a harmless gesture which has captured his imagination. He's not doing it in a piss taking way, he's simply joining in with something I do. But however popular Rod is in here, I have to go through the cover teacher motions, so after taking the register I draw their attention to their English literature text books, in which there are many poems. The problem is I have no instructions other than that. I ask them what they were studying in the last lesson, but there is a conflicting response.

'Love and relationships Sir!'

'No it wasn't, it was power and conflict.'

If I had a list of poems they were supposed to study, I could try and work out which subject is relevant, but I haven't. Someone offers to go and ask their regular teacher, who is in

TAKE COVER!

another classroom (why?), and I gladly despatch her. On her return I'm none the wiser.

'What did he say?'
'He just said carry on, Sir.'

I'm thinking carry on with what?

All I have is a book of ancient poems and no steer as to which ones the teacher is using to teach them. Other than that, all I have at my disposal is a room with some tables and chairs and some vague ideas on how to entertain teenagers who are about to become adults. I have no choice but to let them amuse themselves, but then I've become Mr nice guy again. Anyway, the mobile phones are already out, some with headphones plugged in, others are on Facebook or YouTube or Snapchat. I'm also exhausted and ill inclined to enter into the complex task of getting them to put forbidden stuff away while still remaining a good guy.

But then things take a turn for the worse. For some reason, they seem to be taking particular interest in me. There is much amusement as two or three of them start filming me on their phones. Then they take selfies whilst pointing at me in the background. I can't think why they are doing this, but it's possible they find it amusing because it is evidence that I am letting them get away with using mobile phones in class.

Naughty me!

This is potentially harmful as a cover support teacher (If the word teacher can be suitably applied here) because if they show these little classroom snippets to the wrong people, my days here could well be numbered. Too much Mr Nice Guy could well turn out to be no more Mr Nice Guy.

But the dynamic in the classroom has gone too far to be addressed without me losing a lot of face. I fumble through the rest of the lesson, trying to avoid being filmed while engaging these lively teenagers in conversation to keep some kind of peaceful equilibrium until the bell goes and they're off almost as quickly as they came in.

Oh well, I'm not the right man for the job anyway. I doubt anybody really is to be frank. Then on my way to the bus stop I get a phone call:

SPIKE WEBB

'Hello?'
'Eeeyloh?'
'Who's this?'
'I won learn Eeeengleesh'
'You do, do you?'
'How much for me to learn?'
'thirty pounds an hour'
'Thirty smackers? Don't be a dumb ass – I ain't gonna stay in this shit hole anyway preacher man!'
'Why are you calling me then?'
'Call it a tenner buddy and you got yesself a deal!'
'I really have to go now.'
There are times when almost anything can brighten your day.

FLASHBACK: CLASSROOM RAGE AT THE CLICK OF A BUTTON

When I was at school, surliness was sometimes in evidence but not usually in abundance. Some behaviors were likely to be met with fearful consequences, the severity of which would be difficult to predict, but usually enough to put most people off pushing things too far. Poor conduct, if tolerated, generally manifested itself in the form of humour. Like most teenagers, Grammar School boys can be fairly relentless when they're enjoying and sharing a joke. The butt of the joke would normally be the teacher, especially if that teacher had a reputation for being easily wound up, or a little ineffectual from a discipline point of view.

One such individual had a nickname which we shall refer to here as Percy. He was a French teacher, a nice man but totally unconvincing as a figure of authority. And the poor man paid the price, every day.

On one occasion, during a French lesson, someone had introduced a small, metal clicking device into the proceedings. The idea was to pass this round the room, activating the clicking sound every now and then, so that the audible clicks could be heard at regular intervals from different parts of the room. Even those boys earnestly engaged in the study of the French language as Percy spoke and scribbled on the blackboard did their bit when their turn came around and delivered a quick click before passing it on.

Of course, Percy knew exactly what was going on but ignored it for a while, hoping it would go away. But things like this never go away by themselves, they just get worse until a man's patience is tried too far.

'Ok who's got it?'
'What, Sir?'
'Who's making the clicking noise?'
'What clicking noise, Sir?'
'Someone's got a clicker thing in here and is passing it round the room!'
'We can't hear anything Sir!'

As ever, Percy was beginning to turn a little red with anger.

'Stop the clicking or someone will get into trouble.'

The class knew what tactic to employ and for a while the clicking ceased, just long enough for Percy to think that he had won. To celebrate, he decided to improve our pronunciation skills and told us to repeat sentences after he speaks them:

'Nous sommes dans la salle de classe.'
'Nous sommes dans la salle de classe.'
Silence.
'Nous étudions la langue Français.'
A click from the back of the room.
'Nous étudions la langue Français.'
Silence.
'Nous étudions également comment parler Français.'
A click from the centre of the room.
'Nous étudions également comment parler Français.'
A click from the front left-hand-side.
'Right that's it! Who's got it?'
'Got what, Sir?'
'The clicker, who's got it?'
'What's a clicker, Sir?'
Click from the back again. Percy is shouting now.
'Right, everybody stand up!'
We all stood.

TAKE COVER!

'All of you open your hands!'

We opened our hands and Percy could see that no-one was holding a clicker. He walked around the room checking the desk surfaces, but no clicker. Frustrated almost to boiling point, Percy returned to the front of the class, relieved at least that he had eradicated the clicking sound.

'For the remaining few minutes you will remain standing with your hands open and repeat the sentences:

'Nous avons nous-mêmes se comportera dans la classe.'

'Nous avons nous-mêmes se comportera dans la classe.'

A click from the centre of the room. Someone had placed it under his foot.

This was enough to tip Percy over the edge and the ensuing bellowing was, thankfully for him, halted by the sound of the bell and he made his way somewhat unusually out of the room before everyone else.

Another example of the kind of torment visited upon poor Percy was the humming. It would begin with one person delivering a soft, consistent humming sound. One continuous note, almost as though its source might be electronic. After a while another would join in from another part of the room, not necessarily the same note, but nonetheless equally as consistent with the same sound texture, as though from the same source. Soon another would join in, until a good many people were producing an ever-increasing humming sound. Occasionally we would stop and begin the process again, to give the impression that it was a random, ongoing problem.

Of course, Percy ignored this to start with:

'Some past participles with avoir are irregular...'

'mmmmmmmmmm...'

'For instance, the past participle of boire, which means to drink, is bu...'

'mmmmmmmmmmmmmmmmmm...'

'...and for comprendre, which means to understand, is...'

'mmmmmmmmmmmmmmmmmmmmmm...'

SPIKE WEBB

'COMPRIS! RIGHT WHO'S HUMMING! STOP THE HUMMING!'

'It's the lights, Sir!'

'What lights?'

'The long fluorescent lights hanging from the ceiling, Sir!'

'Don't be ridiculous. No more humming!'

Once again, the class know how to play the game and hang back for a while.

'Right repeat after me: Nous apprenons à parler français.'

'Nous apprenons à parler français.'

'Bientôt, nous serons en mesure de parler français.'

'Bientôt, nous serons en mesure de parler français.'

'Nous aimerions apprendre Français ensemble.'

'mmmmmmmmmm…'

'Nous aimerions apprendre Français ensemble.'

'mmmmmmmmmmmmmmmmm…'

'THE HUMMING'S STARTED! STOP THE HUMMING!'

'It's the lights, Sir!'

'mmmmmmmmmm…'

Red faced in rage, Percy marched over to the light switch by the classroom door and switched off the lights, at which point the humming completely stopped. This worked for a while, but as the afternoon lesson progressed, the room became darker, so Percy had to switch the lights back on. And no prizes for predicting what happened next.

The levels of cruelty jointly deployed by young teenagers can reach almost inhuman proportions. Had Percy simply ignored the clicking, pretending that he couldn't actually hear it, the class may have got bored. However, It's more likely that it would simply have got even worse so that Percy had no choice but to react. Part of me did feel sorry for him, but peer pressure is high at that age, and because he's a grown up, you assume he'll be OK. The truth is, he probably wasn't.

I bumped into Percy in my local Sainsbury's many years later, long after I had left school and he had retired. He

TAKE COVER!

was at the checkout in the queue next to me. He smiled and mouthed a hello, and I returned the gesture. We couldn't chat as items were being scanned and the hustle and bustle of bag filling and payment processes was at hand, but I'd have liked the chance to ask him how he was. Apologise even.

That was the last I saw of Percy, a nice, gentle man who simply couldn't control a class.

A MOMENT IN TIME

It's Saturday afternoon and I'm walking up my local High Street with my wife. We're talking about our past week, the ups and downs, what to expect on Monday. I tell her I'm worried about bumping into Jack again. The guy who doesn't seem to have any sense of peace about him. The explosive, unpredictable one who can just turn at any time. I've been wondering about what chances are ever going to be in store for him.

    We come upon a bit of street theatre at the top of the town. It's part of a youth arts festival. People are milling around, some watching in deck chairs. We decide to take a look and sit on a stone wall near the actors. Sad but beautiful music is playing. There is a huge, 30 feet high funnel with an opening at the top and a rope dangling to the ground. Below are dozens of discarded luggage bags and old clothes. A man is kneeling on the ground a few yards in front of this, fiddling with his own battered suitcase. He is black with colourful painted lines on his face and dressed in flowing rags. He opens the bag, closes it, looks around him as if having arrived in a completely unknown place. He looks lost, but it is as though he expected to be. He seems resigned to something. A kind of loneliness.

    Wandering around behind him is a young woman, white but with similar painted lines on her face. She is lost too. As I'm thinking they must have appeared at the top of the funnel and climbed down, the woman approaches the man and hands him what looks like a biscuit or wafer. He takes it slowly

TAKE COVER!

and puts it to his mouth, nodding gratefully as she wanders away, towards us. The music is very moving, tragic yet calm. Another man appears at the top of the funnel, rubbing his eyes. He climbs down the rope and dusts himself down. He too has his face painted and is dressed in rags. He looks slightly more purposeful though, and after some wandering about, he ends up over at the nearby cash point which happens to be on the post office wall. He fumbles about there with some apparent difficulty, then walks off in another direction.

While all this is happening, almost at random, some people are watching, intrigued. Others are simply carrying on with their day, glancing as they pass by. Some mums and dads stop to look with their children in tow. They have ice creams and are making some noise like kids do. Some teenage lads are hanging about, smoking, showing off, a bit like some of the students at school. Strangely enough, one of them looks a tiny bit like Jack. As life goes on around them in real time, these characters from the funnel continue to look lost. And the more they are ignored, the better the effect of their loneliness and disorientation.

Then the woman kneels a couple of yards in front of us. She takes from a tattered shoulder bag a pair of children's shoes, about the size that might fit a one year old. She looks wistfully up at the sky, then bowing her head she slowly does up the tiny buckles on the shoes. She takes a drink from a small water bottle and then pours a little water over her eyes, which now appear to be wet with tears. Then, using a piece of her ragged dress, she wipes some moisture from her eyes and begins to polish the tiny shoes. It is as if she is polishing the child's shoes with her tears.

I glance at my wife, who has tears in her eyes. I am a little tearful too. The woman looks up and, noticing this, approaches slowly and gently offers the shoes to my wife, who takes them, smiles at them and says quietly as she hands them back:

'I hope it has a happy ending.'

The woman takes them and nods sympathetically before wandering away.

TAKE COVER!

It is a moment in time that I will never forget. I figure that we've been under quite a bit of pressure recently. Nothing too out of the ordinary, but things have been building up. My wife's been concerned about money, she's been needing a holiday for some time but we can't afford one. I've been unemployed for a while until this cover support teaching which I find stressful. My stepson has just split up with his girlfriend who lived with us for a couple of years, and we miss her too. And there's been the EU Referendum. And we've seen pictures of helpless people clinging to capsized boats, fleeing in terror from far-off lands. And, like so many, we're worried about bills. As the lady with the tiny shoes moves to the other side of the street, another character appears in rags at the opening of the funnel.

We've got things to do, so we get up to go. As we walk away, I'm thinking how sometimes all it takes is something you happen upon by accident, completely at random, to trigger a release of worries, stresses, sadness, all at once. Then my wife tells me more about those tears.

Some of them were for the child we never had.

SHELL SHOCK

It's Friday afternoon and I'm knackered. It's been a gruelling day, featuring the likes of various excitable characters who have featured from time to time in these pages so far; loose cannons, uncontrollable water bottle flipping 11-year-olds, surly GCSE students who've realised they have little chance of passing their exams, and some noise levels that can bring a person to the point of insanity.

In fact, the insanity of it all has driven me to adopt a resigned, staring pose. I'm looking straight ahead, slightly mad, and slightly amused. After all, it's near the end of term and the summer holidays are approaching. The class of thirty or so 14/15-year-olds is boisterous and excitable. However they quieten down when they see the somewhat unusual stance I have adopted.

Continuing to stare straight ahead, seemingly possessed, I address the class thus:

'Mr Brearson cannot be here this afternoon, as a consequence of which, I am. My name is Mr Webb, and I am disinclined to raise my voice, which means the cumulative volume in this room shall be no greater than that of the syllables you are hearing now. This will continue for fifty-five minutes.'

There is a snigger, but I don't falter.

'It is without doubt one of the greatest privileges known to man, to be the recipient of knowledge imparted willingly by another. When such deliverances are enjoyed en masse, it should be considered one of the Almighty's most magnanimous of indulgencies.'

More sniggering.

'Regrettably, this cannot be one of those occasions. Why? Because I am sadly unable to adopt the position of one who can furnish you with academic enlightenment with regard to the study of Geography.

'However, I do not intend to simply sit down on that chair and ignore you. That would be rude. And I am not a rude man.'

Giggles. I continue to stare insanely ahead.

'I see you have your text books ready for opening at page 74 for the purpose of quiet and reflective study. It would also be equally rude of me to come around and bully you into doing something I can't even do myself!

'So we're going to have to come to an arrangement which is mutually agreeable to you as a collective, and myself as an individual. That arrangement shall be as follows.'

They are all ears now.

'You will voluntarily pay some meaningful attention to your text books for sixty percent of our remaining time together. The other forty percent will be spent in casual but earnest discussion, both amongst yourselves and with myself on matters various, but unrelated to the study of geography. Upon the successful deployment of this initiative reaching thirty minutes, other privileges will be introduced into the proceedings. You may begin to play music privately on your mobile phones via headphones, sedaciously and in the manner of one who is enjoying quiet reflection.'

This is met with some enthusiasm.

And then with a smile:

'Do we have a deal?'

'Yes, Sir!'

During the course of my meandering around the room, most of the students at least fake the appearance of active study, but as time progresses I'm happy to chat normally with them about this and that. I make it quite clear that I am in fact normal and my disciplinary delivery was a way of creating an

TAKE COVER!

equilibrium – plus I was having a bit of fun, sending myself up. But the thing is it has worked. Resigning myself to a state of tired, pompous delirium seems to have presented the class with something unexpected, and actually doing a deal with them has worked better than trying to shut them up.

But this has been a lucky occasion. The class were responsive; it's Leaton Down School which is generally a bit easier than some of the others. And I've learned something: behave as if you're slightly mad, pompous and quietly confident as though nothing could possibly faze you, sending yourself up ever-so-slightly and it might just do the trick.

It's also good practice for your acting career.

ARMISTICE DAY – PEACE AT LEAST

It's the last lesson of the day. And it could well be my last lesson of the term, possibly my last lesson of all. I'm covering religious Studies for an hour. The students are all year 10, soon to become Year 11 after the summer break. They have just completed their mock GCSEs for this year, so now they are relaxed, almost grown-up, and, for now, happy. They have been writing a diary, called 'My Life's Journey', which I have asked them to continue with today, whilst chatting quietly of course.

I haven't met these students before as it's Abbey Cross, the big one I've only been to occasionally. I can tell they seem to like me though, as I chat with them occasionally while strolling round the room. I addressed the class slightly differently today:

'Hello, my name is Mr Webb, but you can call me Rod Stewart.'

They laugh a little, as I hoped they would. Because after all this time, I still want to be liked.

So as they chat amongst themselves, filling in their diaries when they feel like it, I'm thinking what a peaceful time this is. All seems to be in harmony. A room full of people who have found mutual respect on their journey into whatever the future holds. They all have dreams, some big, some small, but all equally as important. And they have time, time to make the

TAKE COVER!

best of what they can. Part of me worries for them. It's that 'back of the head' thing again.

And I want their dreams to work for them, just like I want mine to work for me. I'm worried because I wonder if this little journal of mine is ever really going to become a memoir or a book. I worry that no-one will want to read It anyway at the end of the day. Why should anyone be interested? I worry that all this writing could actually be a waste of time.

I decide to take another turn around the room. I'm captivated by the posters and pictures on the walls of the classroom. They are clearly part of a course of religious and social study. There are some news cuttings:

A photo of a Muslim and a Jew playing tennis, defying hate to play mixed doubles.

There is a shrouded figure dishing up a plate of food and a caption which says that Britons are turning to the Sikh community for food.

An ancient newspaper cutting tells the story of a negro woman called Park who changed a nation by refusing to stand for a white man on a bus. She is quoted as saying:

'I had no idea it would turn into this – it was an ordinary day, just like any other day.'

And then there is Diana, Princess of Wales, bending down to shake the hand of Mother Teresa, with a line that says however different their own paths and skills are, they must strive to make the world a better place.

Then, I come upon a display of hand-drawn posters by younger students, probably eleven or twelve-year-olds. The theme is 'The last piece of paper'. It's what you would write to the world as a final message if you were the person with the last piece of paper. One catches my eye and I can't stop looking at it. There is a tiny, coloured globe – planet earth. Next to this is a large, beautifully drawn, old-fashioned open book. There is a cross drawn on the parchment, and underneath is written:

'Keep your dreams and all that mankind created for us. Don't give up.'

SPIKE WEBB

Sometimes the best advice comes when you least expect it.

ON LEAVE AT LAST

It's the end of term and the end of my journey. I've fought the last battle and I'm on the bus, on my way home for the last time. So I'm looking back at this last three months or so, and what, if anything, I may have achieved. Over and above paying bills and buying Guinness that is.

There were occasions when I really thought I'd won. I'd be sitting on the bus on my way home, congratulating myself on keeping a classroom fairly quiet and free from the rigours of battle, with just the odd bit of random shelling and occasional gunfire.

But the truth is, you can't win. And to be fair, neither can they. In some classrooms, nobody wins. Those who aren't interested are wasting their time. Cover teachers like me who try and force their interest are wasting their time. And the few who are interested in algebra, or geography, or Romeo and Juliet, or at least getting past the necessary GCSE, can never win because often their progress is terminally stunted by the behaviour of those who just don't want to know. Of course, you do get cover lesson classes in which there are memorable, worthwhile moments, some moving, harrowing even, some hilarious and others truly bizarre. And at the end of the day, children and teenagers are the best entertainers.

In three months of life as a cover support teacher in secondary schools, I've learned more myself than I thought possible. I learned that going in head first with romantic aspirations of changing their outlook on academic life is like attempting a builder's clean with a dish cloth from Pound Land.

But I also learned a lot about the tools of the trade. Use your voice carefully, keeping it at a forceful but respectful level. Increase the volume sparingly, so that when you do, it means something. Talking loudly from the start simply encourages your class to assume that is the benchmark volume for the whole lesson and they will match it automatically.

And smile. It doesn't hurt to smile occasionally. You're not really a robot, or a pre-programmed fighting machine. You're human, just like they are. In the grand scheme of things, you're not much different. Huge though the difference in age is, and however further you've come along life's travels, the truth is, you share the same helping of troubles, fears, tears, laughter, joy and disappointment. In as much as you want them to respect you for what you already know and have learned about life, respect them for what they have yet to know and learn. For the chances are they will have just as hard a time getting there as you did. And the way the world is changing, it will be even harder for them.

But I've discovered something that I never thought would happen. I've been given the opportunity to meet the old me. The schoolboy from years ago I thought I'd forgotten about. These people have reminded me of all the fears, phobias, worries, ambitions and youthful torment that went with growing up. And I've also discovered that a lot of my insecurities have never really gone away. Perhaps they never do. Maybe we just get better at hiding them.

And somewhere deep inside, I've grown to love these people. Ok, so I'm not qualified to teach them properly or influence their academic development, but somewhere along the line I've discovered that I actually do care. Not just about the kids, but about the teachers and teaching assistants who work so hard to try and get the best out of them. But as we've seen, their hands are tied.

And it's forced me to wonder about what I've done since I started big school. Since I went from a shy, hiding, high-voiced eleven-year-old to a hippy worshipping, eccentric bin-

TAKE COVER!

bashing teenaged drummer to the beer drinking pseudo-intellect who passed his O and A level GCSEs. From turning down a university place to try and become a rock star, ten years in the Civil Service followed by a touch of good fortune that led to a good career in advertising. Then redundancy, freelancing, cleaning jobs here and there and all this against a backdrop of drumming, drumming and more drumming.

And all the personal stuff. A happy but childless marriage, divorce, an even happier marriage with two now grown up step kids. And desperate to pay some bills and take the person who is my wife and best friend on a short break to Brighton, I have come to a place that has taken me all the way back to the beginning, to where I started. And as I tried pompously to tell my first class of 15-year-olds on my first day, this is where it starts.

From my position at the back of the bus I can see a sea of heads, mostly students of different ages, all on their way to whatever their lives will become. Exams, the torment of growing up but staying young, planning a future with whatever pot of opportunities they may have, big or small.

And ultimately, they are on their way to finding out about their hopes and dreams: the difference between those that really can come true, and those that can truly never be.

For my part, tough though it has been, I wouldn't have missed this opportunity for the world. Because I've learned far more from these people than they could possibly have learned from me. But I hope they liked me, as a person. Just as much as I wanted to be liked at school all those years ago. At the end of the day, nothing much has changed.

One thing's for sure, my Mum would have loved it. She was a great teacher in a multitude of ways. And I get the feeling that, wherever she is now, she wanted me to do this. Because it has become so much more than paying the bills. It's been one of the most important tests I've ever taken.

I hope I passed.

ROLLING DOWN THAT HILL

I'm wandering out of the entrance to a place called Hunton Park, where I got married twelve years ago. I've been coming to the lounge area here with my laptop for a few weeks to put together the finishing touches to this little book; this little book about not so little people – people who have lots of worries about the future, and the people who worry about them.

And I'm worried. Is it any good? Will it get published? Will anybody read it? Like it?

As I walk up the steps to the long drive, where my wedding guests gathered all those years ago, I pass two children, a boy of about five and his sister of about four. They're having great fun together, rolling down a damp grass verge. Mum is watching them, in loving exasperation. She wants to leave, but they are in heaven.

'Come on darlings! Time to go home now…'

'Oh, go on Mummy – just one more time! Please?'

So she lets them play on for a while. I smile as I pass by. And as I leave them behind I'm musing. If there is a heaven, maybe it could be that you go back to one of your happiest moments, free of worry and care, when time simply stops and you get to roll down that grass verge as many times as you want, while Mum watches over you, forever.

THE LAST POST

I'm sitting at the back of a bus on the old route I used to take home from one of the schools I used to work in. I've been visiting a friend who happens to live nearby. We come to a routine stop and a few school kids get on. It's that time of day, mid-afternoon and school's out. A young teenage lad takes the seat in front of me. He's not in school uniform, but I recognise him as he turns to me:

'Hi Sir, do you remember me? You used to take some of my maths lessons.'

'Yes I do.'

'Sorry I was so noisy.'

'That's ok. What are you up to these days?'

He tells me that he's going to college to study IT and then he wants to start his own business support company. He's full of energy and I can see in his eyes he's excited about the future. He also tells me he wants to rent somewhere with his girlfriend as soon as he gets a part time evening job, then maybe buy somewhere when the business takes off. I'm happy for him as he allows his dreams to beckon him on into the battlefields that lie ahead.

He has all the hope and courage of a young man about to make his way in the world. I wish him all the luck in the world as we come to his stop:

'Thank you Sir, nice to see you again!'

And with that he jumps off the bus and waves before sauntering off into his future.

SPIKE WEBB

They say that the eyes are the windows to the soul. But I reckon if you want to see someone's soul laid bare for all to see...

...watch them as they walk away.

EPILOGUE

March, 2020. Unexpectedly, I've found myself temporarily back in the schools, and I'm taking the register in a year 9 class at Gatesbury, where the mood is a combination of sombre and flippant.

'Josh?'
'Here, Sir.'
'Lily?'
'Here, Sir'
'Jacob?'
(A few shout out):
'He's self-isolating with a cold, Sir'
'Olivia?'
'Here, Sir.'
'Hailey?'
'Isolation, Sir!'
'Ryan?'
(exaggerated enthusiasm):
'Here, SIR!!'
'Jack?'
'Here, Sir.'
'Sophia?'
(collective drone):
'Coronavirus!'
'Noah?'
'Here, Sir.'
'Ethan?'

(collective drone):
'Coronavirus!'
'Grace?'
(silly voice):
'Heeeere, Sir.'
'Kayla?'
'Here, Sir!'
'Connor?'
(collective drone):
'Coronavirus!'
Well, you get the picture.

I hadn't intended to write this epilogue when this little book was almost complete a few months ago. However, due to recent events I felt compelled to add a short note. After finishing my two terms as cover teacher in 2016, I took a permanent writing job, completely unconnected with teaching or education, until I was made redundant at the end of 2019. This led to me going back into the schools as a cover teacher. This was at the same time that the coronavirus pandemic was developing, so my return to cover work only lasted until the schools were finally closed after about a month.

Back in the schools, what I encountered was roughly the same as before. Nothing much had changed in four years; the difficulties with discipline, the almost anarchic nature of the cover periods (or most of them) and the sense of futility about it all still prevailed.

But of course, I'm referring to cover lessons here, not proper lessons with real teachers. As I've said before, the very nature of my role as cover support has meant that I had little or no exposure to any proper lessons. However, for what it's worth, as somebody who has had very little training or experience in real teaching, that which I did witness was highly impressive. The professionals tasked with the education of teenagers to GCSE level are up against so much these days, no wonder their skills are challenged. I have since spoken to members of my family who are working in education and it seems they are under such enormous pressure to constantly prove themselves by doing stuff other than actually teaching

TAKE COVER!

that they simply buckle under the strain. Many are working twelve-hour days that render the sound of the home time bell almost irrelevant, simply to put a tick in a box that says you can keep your job, for the time being.

So, all work and no play makes Jack a sick boy.

I don't know who decides that teachers should be under such monumental pressure to jump through so many bureaucratic hoops as opposed to concentrating on what they are actually good at, teaching. Having returned briefly to the schools, once again it's obvious that there should be no need for people like me. And the students know this too – especially the older ones. So, of course they feel short changed. Then there are all the other elements like lack of social discipline and the constant arrival of ever-changing technologies that mean they are even harder to control. Add to that the fact that they like to have a bit of a laugh and you have a recipe for disaster.

One thing I noticed was that the rewards and consequences charts that I moaned about earlier in this book have disappeared from the classroom walls. On asking a year nine student what had happened to them, I was told that students now access their rewards and consequences accounts on the school intranet. I assume that's a step in the right direction as at least the charts are no longer on permanent display as a constant reminder that the authorities have failed to maintain ownership of an adequate disciplinary system; something which traditionally harboured a healthy degree of mystery and fear which was not negotiable and certainly didn't manifest itself in a kind of game.

Anyway, what would I know? I'm not in any way qualified to give advice on the best way to discipline students. But I was there, in the thick of it for two-and-a-bit terms, and as a consequence, I am qualified to say what I saw and give an opinion.

But what happens when teenagers are returned to school after lockdown and are told to observe social distancing rules? They will presumably be sitting two metres apart. That's nearly seven feet! That's a long way for people who tend to thrive on close communication, especially when they are engaged in rebellious or conspiratorial bonding. They won't be able to steal pens anymore. They won't be able to giggle together anymore. And forget play-fighting, or even real fighting. They will be completely exposed as individuals. They'll just have to knuckle down to good old Romeo and Juliet. Who would have thought that, the disciplinary system having failed so dismally, it would take a deadly virus to keep them quiet?

One thing's for sure, there will be more paper airplanes flying around than ever before.

Printed in Great Britain
by Amazon